CONTOURS

CONTOURS

THE COURSES BEHIND REMARKABLE GOLF ADVENTURES

WILLIAM WATT

Hardie Grant
BOOKS

Cape Kidnappers and Barnbougle Dunes proved destination golf could work down under.

FOREWORD

BY TOM DOAK

I first landed in Australia on 3 March 1988. I remember the date only because the immigration officer loudly announced, 'The date is 3/3, even you Americans can't get it wrong.' I was in the midst of building my first solo design and as the project was under snow in Michigan, I thought it would be great to get to the Sandbelt and try to learn what great bunkers looked like. I'd been struggling to get the shapes right.

I didn't know if I would ever get back that way, so I gave myself three weeks in Australia and a week to see New Zealand, as sort of an afterthought. Amazingly, because I had been writing for *Golf Magazine* as a side gig in the United States, I was in contact with a couple of Aussies who were on the panel to rate the top-100 courses in the world, who offered to host me. This led to a friendship with Tom Ramsey, the late golf writing legend, and a memorable dinner at Richie Benaud's apartment in Coogee on my second day in the country.

I spent a few days in Sydney getting my bearings, three days in Adelaide during the Festival, and then a good ten days in the Sandbelt, seeing everything I'd heard of except Woodlands. All the best courses were in the suburbs. I never saw a kangaroo or wallaby that first trip, except at the zoo – though I did make the pilgrimage to Barwon Heads, where the late Bud Russell played with me, and even went down to the Mornington Peninsula to see a brand-new course called The National. Mostly, I was mesmerised with The Royal Melbourne, and impressed with the work that Kingston Heath superintendent, Graeme Grant, had carried out to improve his course.

En route home, I stopped in New Zealand, which wasn't considered a golf destination at the time. Titirangi, Paraparaumu, Wairakei and Rotorua were the only courses I'd heard of, but I thought I should see the countryside. I never had an inkling that it would play such a meaningful part in my life. Over the years, I've made thirty-three trips back to build my three golf courses, or occasionally to stop in and play them on my way to Oz.

Luckily, just as my reputation was starting to grow in the late 1990s, so was golf development in Australia and New Zealand. My first foray was to interview to build one of the two new courses at The National in 1998, but Peter Thomson and Greg Norman were both Australians who had won The Open, and I wasn't and hadn't, so that was that. A year later, David Inglis asked if I would be interested in building a course down the road at St Andrews Beach and I jumped at the chance, though he abandoned the project when the local council wouldn't grant zoning for residential property to help pay for the land acquisition.

In 2000, we built Pacific Dunes in Oregon, and my reputation went from being a designer with 'potential' to someone who made the most of beautiful land. But it's harder to get permission to build on beautiful land in America than it is down your way, because there are more people around to object to 'growth'. So in the year after Pacific Dunes opened, my first calls to work on great land were from Cape Kidnappers in New Zealand, and then Barnbougle Dunes in Tasmania. Then Mike Clayton asked if I'd like to work with a new developer at St Andrews Beach. We built all of those courses, back-to-back, in 2002–03.

The success of Cape Kidnappers – building on David Harman's Kauri Cliffs and Barnbougle followed by Lost Farm – was just as good for golf development in the two countries as it was for my career. Prior to that, there was much doubt in Australia that a course outside of the big cities could be successful. Barnbougle proved it could happen, opening the way for the resort's expansion and for further developments on King Island. The success of Cape Kidnappers proved that US and UK visitors would travel that far for destination golf, which led to the development of high-end courses in Queenstown, and later to Tara Iti and the new resort down the beach.

Better yet, because those courses were all open to the public, the golf magazines published photos of them around the world. No matter how far away they were, readers could conceivably go play them, which they couldn't do at the other great course of its generation: Sand Hills in Nebraska. So the boom in resort and public golf has also led to a greater interest in golf course design. Forty years ago, I had to go through an inter-library loan to find a copy of Alister MacKenzie's book. Now, every book on design has been reprinted and you can get it in two clicks from Amazon, and there are hours and hours of podcasts and website interviews with me and other modern designers.

This book you're holding shows just how far we've come – from technical manuals hidden away in libraries to rich explorations of how these courses came to be. If you have even a passing interest in the topic, you may easily be lured into the depths.

Don't say I didn't warn you.

CONTENTS

Superintendent Brian Palmer cutting pins at Tara Iti

'Golf is a game, and talk and discussion is all to the interests of the game. Anything that keeps the game alive and prevents us being bored with it is an advantage. Anything that makes us think about it, talk about it and dream about it is all to the good and prevents the game becoming dead.'

DR ALISTER MACKENZIE

INTRODUCTION

WORDS AND PHOTOGRAPHY
BY WILLIAM WATT

Experiencing a true epiphany is a little like getting a hole-in-one. Unexpected. Instantaneous. Permanent. Euphoric. Rare. Unlike those small revelations we all have – like finally realising your alignment was off after months of wayward drives – a genuine epiphany rewrites your mental hard drive completely. One minute you're trudging along in familiar territory, the next you're blinking in the fierce light of a new reality. Most of us will experience perhaps three or four of these cosmic downloads in our lifetime, if we're lucky. Some poor souls will go through life thinking their latest Instagram insight counts as enlightenment, never knowing what they've missed.

These lightbulb moments aren't just metaphorical – they're an actual rewiring of our brains in real-time. Unlike the usual slow grind of learning a new piece of software or perfecting your putting stroke, an epiphany creates new neural pathways in an instant. It's as if your brain suddenly discovers a shortcut through territory you never knew existed. No wonder these moments feel so euphoric – and that they tend to stay with us for good.

I experienced just such an epiphany the first time I stood on the 10th tee at The Royal Melbourne Golf Club. Looking out over the audacious dogleg bunker at the flag waving temptingly at me, almost within range, it hit me right between the eyes. The instant my ball smashed into the top lip of the bunker a deeper world of golf, previously obscured from view, opened up before me.

I had played golf for most of my life and thought I had experienced all the highs and lows this great game can bring (although I still haven't experienced the aforementioned euphoria of a hole-in-one). But I didn't know golf could do *that*. At that moment, I knew – this was *the* game for the rest of my life.

Weeks later, I was still thinking about that 10th hole – where I needed to hit my drive next time to play the hole strategically, making the most of the ground contours, while balancing the risk of the chasmic bunker. Where the best layup shot would be, depending how my swing was feeling, the wind direction, time of year, the lie and the pin position that day. Areas to avoid at all costs, and areas that should be ok, even in case of a mis-hit. Before long, I moved on to the short par-3 16th, which was just as interesting. I still think about these same holes today, sometimes late at night, more than twelve years after the 10th took my number.

Until that day, I had mainly focused on my own golf game – head down, worrying about swing mechanics, my score or the gear in my oversized golf bag. That morning, my reality shifted forever. My gaze had been lifted from the turf right in front of me to the contours beyond. From worrying about my game and getting caught in the details to enjoying the moment I was in, where I was, who I was with and what I could perceive of the world around me.

Today, I can barely keep a scorecard, and rarely do. I am too taken with the feast for the senses all around me to be distracted by writing down a number. The look of the ground contours at sunset, a peek through the trees at a future hole on the routing, or the flight of a stinger against a mountain backdrop. The sounds of the crashing waves, the local birdlife or a driver echoing through pine trees. The comforting smell of a damp forest, or of fresh salty air, or springtime heath. Feeling the cushioning of the turf beneath my feet, the crisp dimples of a new golf ball, the compression of a well-hit 6-iron. The taste of victory, often in the form of a dram of single malt whiskey from a flask buried in my golf bag, warming our chests on a cold winter's day after holing a long birdie putt.

All this is what I want *Contours* to be for you – a ticket to enjoying the greatest game in the world on a whole new level. From being a golfer who looks down at the turf, at your equipment or your scorecard to one who looks up and soaks it all in. From someone who experiences frustration if they are playing poorly to one who knows, deep down, that it doesn't really matter. From seeing a golf course merely as a technical challenge to appreciating the artistry, strategy and unique character of the land itself – what wine lovers call terroir – and the very ground you are standing on. And, perhaps most importantly, to 'think about it, dream about it and talk about it' with those whom you're lucky enough to experience it with.

LEFT The intimidating, tempting and memorable par-4 10th at Royal Melbourne West

ROUTING THE COURSE

WORDS BY MIKE COCKING
PHOTOGRAPHY BY BJ SHULTZ

'There are 118 holes out here.
All I have to do is eliminate the 100.'

PERRY MAXWELL

Roughed-in fairways at Tepetonka, Minnesota, United States

The ultimate test for a golf course architect is the routing. Deciding how to traverse the property and what journey the golfer will take from the 1st tee to the 18th green. It's a complex process that sometimes comes together quickly, or, just as often, demands months of study and multiple site visits. The challenge lies not just in finding great holes, but in the knowledge that there's no single correct answer. Show a routing plan to five different architects and you'll get five different layouts, each believing theirs to be the best. There might be dozens of ways to route a course, and no one is there to tell you if and when you've solved the puzzle. It is perhaps this lack of knowing that is the most difficult aspect of all – it simply comes down to the architect in question deciding which one stands above all others.

The Art and Science of Routing

In essence, the architect's aim in routing a golf course is to try to get the most out of the natural assets of a property. This might mean capturing a great view, a stretch of ocean, following a river or creek, utilising dune-land or just making the most of brilliantly crumpled ground. If the land is good enough, laying out the holes should also help minimise the amount of dirt to move, with the added advantage that you will inevitably find some unique holes through the process.

If you're lucky, the site may have multiple landscapes that allow the architect to weave in and out of different parts of the property throughout the round. The trick is to avoid using these features all at once – ideally you will come to and return to them multiple times during the journey. Cypress Point provides a great example of this, with holes weaving in and out of the sand dunes and wooded sections of the property, before finishing with a thrilling stretch of holes along the ocean.

So, where to begin?

First, I should point out there really is no right and wrong. Different architects work in different ways and have differing views on what they believe is great golf. Pretty much anyone can gaze out into the distance and see a nice-looking hole through the valleys and ridges of a new property. It doesn't take years of working in design to see something – just a bit of imagination. The real challenge lies in finding eighteen of them: eighteen holes with a variety of lengths, orientations, tee shots and green sites. Eighteen holes that work seamlessly and integrate as a group. Eighteen holes that are good enough to make someone want to come back and play them again and again.

When the game was evolving, architects were bound by the contours of the land to a far greater extent than today. Holes had to be cleverly routed over the property simply because they didn't have the equipment to do otherwise. This left us with some wonderfully unique and often quirky designs. In addition, architects were much less concerned with what others thought was acceptable. They were pushing the boundaries and happy to take risks. Breaking the conventional thinking is sometimes the best way to maximise a property's natural attributes.

This type of thinking can present in different ways. Perhaps the site is best suited to a shorter course – say closer to 6,500 yards than the more common 7,500, which most clubs seem to chase. Or maybe the ground conditions suit a high number of par-3s and the overall par is only 68 or 69. Maybe a section of the property features some dramatic dunes and warrants consecutive par-3s, or perhaps the opposite is the case: a long stretch of flat ground where two par-5s in a row will get it over with as quickly as possible. Or maybe playing a blind hole unlocks a brilliant section of the routing. Even more controversially, perhaps a crossover hole adds length to a small site, as it did for MacKenzie at Alwoodley.

As golf course design entered the modern era, there was less and less quirk. Golf courses became increasingly standardised and predictable. Sometimes this was the result of the developer, but other times it was the architect's own design bias. Maybe the owner didn't like blind shots, or perhaps, as a public course, it required returning nines. Balancing these types of requirements without losing the character of the course, or restricting your creativity, was quite the battle. Fortunately, today, many developers understand that design freedom is important, and established architects are afforded a degree of autonomy in deciding their routing.

Tools and Techniques

Learning to read a topographic plan is important. To the untrained eye, these might look like pages full of scribble, but to the experienced, these lines provide a clear view of the site's contours – its valleys, hills, ridges and ravines. Learning to read a 'topo' just needs a bit of practice. Once you've figured out the highs and lows, and understand that the closer together the contour lines are, the steeper the ground (and, conversely, the wider apart, the flatter), you're well on your way.

As you spend more time studying these plans, you start to see the page in three dimensions, much like the magic-eye books that were all the rage in the 1990s. Then, out of the scribbles, you may start to see which parts of the property look like they might make for interesting golf – maybe that's some intriguing fairway contour or perhaps a natural-looking green site.

Being able to read a topo also allows you to assess a big property quickly. With a few days of study, an accomplished architect can look over a few hundred acres and gain an intimate understanding of the features of the property, and perhaps even draw out a bunch of possible golf holes. At this early stage, it's best to keep the 'holes' as simple as possible. Detail such as fairway shapes and bunkers can come later.

But perhaps an architect's most useful tool in the routing process is a good memory. The power to recall hundreds of great holes from around the world can allow you to assess the potential of new land, as well as serving as inspiration. Being able to remember the great holes – be they in plans or in person – can provide a terrific starting point. It's not about copying the design but knowing that a hole of that type will work well across the piece of land in question.

On flatter sites, the architect will tend to focus on the more interesting parts of the property. The little valleys or ridges will add interest to a fairway landing zone or a green site. Wilder, more undulating land can present the opposite problem, requiring a search for the flatter parts for fairways and greens. As a general rule, green sites with more than five per cent slope will be problematic. Likewise, fairways with greater than ten per cent of fall will require major earthworks to create flat areas and avoid balls rolling off into the rough. Although this is somewhat dependent on the choice of grass and time of year (dormant couch, for instance, can behave like a skating rink in winter when cut short, so may require less slope, whereas with lush bentgrass, you can get away with a little more).

> 'An architect's most useful tool in the routing process is a good memory. The power to recall hundreds of great holes from around the world can allow you to assess the potential of new land, as well as serving as inspiration.'

OCM's routing plan for Arm End in Hobart, Tasmania

Arm End, near Hobart in Tasmania, with OCM's routing roughed in

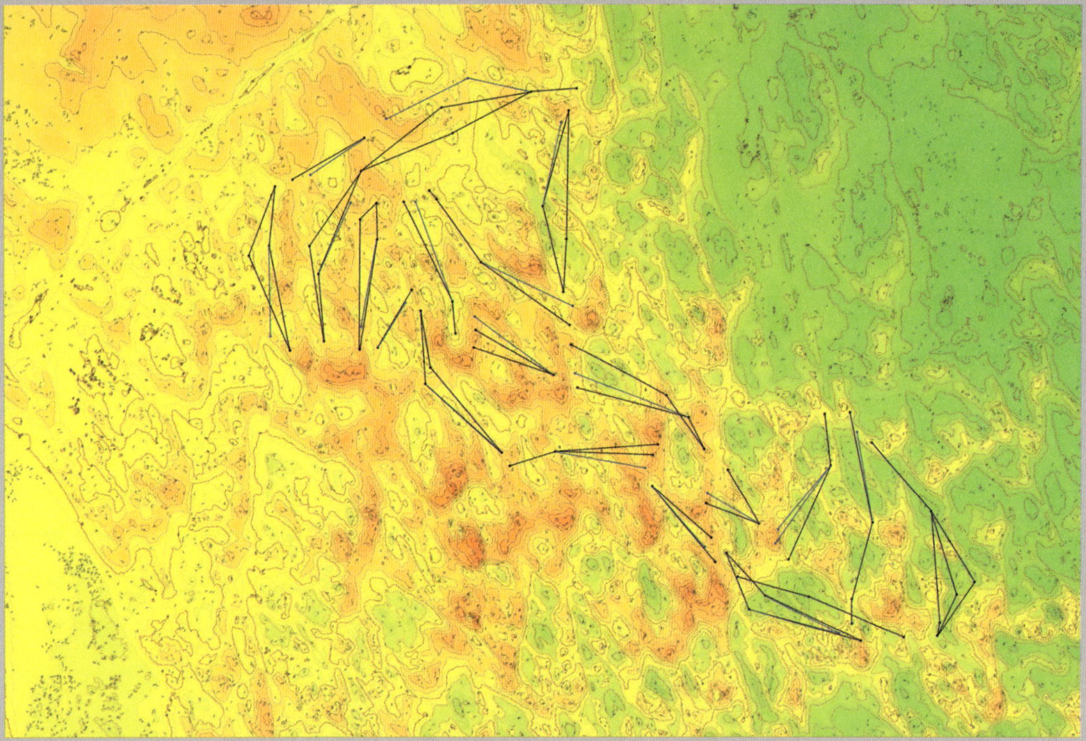

Initial routing options at Tepetonka

Of course, the ideal property sits somewhere in between. Some nice broad hills spaced wide enough to allow for holes to play between ridgelines or across the top of them, but not so tall that it leads to a lot of hill climbing. Fifty- or sixty-foot dunes and ridgelines are perfect. On top of this, there should be enough small-scale movement to add variety in both stance and how the ball reacts upon landing. Some days, a well-played shot may catch an upslope and stop quickly. Other days, you catch a downslope and gain the advantage of twenty or thirty metres of extra roll. Judging where to land and flight your shot provides an additional challenge and rewards the considered and skilful player. Interestingly, on these types of great sites, it's easy to imagine par-4s and par-5s, with the undulations spaced apart to make for great-looking tee shots and approaches. On sites where the undulations are more severe, everything looks like a great par-3.

There are some things that a topographic plan won't reveal: ground conditions, soil type, vegetation, exposed sand or rock and, of course, the views, both within the property and outside the golf course. Is there an ugly building or powerline lying just outside the property boundary or, on a positive note, perhaps views of the water or a spectacular mountain range?

While the process for routing a course hasn't changed much for more than a hundred years, there are a few pieces of modern technology that certainly help. Using CAD design software, we can create a 'heat map' of the topography, which makes it easy to spot the highs and lows of a site. Usually we use cool blue and purple tones to indicate lows, and warm tones like orange and red to show the highs. Other modern technology useful for routing is the GPS and hiking apps, which allow us to track our walks across a site and record comments relating to the ground conditions, be they good, such as 'great green site', or bad, like 'wet ground to be avoided'. On heavily treed properties where visibility is an issue, this can be especially useful and helps the routing process when back in the office.

Of course, others may do it differently. I've seen some architects cut scaled-down golf holes out of paper and arrange them on a plan. Others prefer to walk the site multiple times and then start laying out holes in the field. This could be because they can't read a topographic plan or they just find it better to visualise the holes in the field. But the advantage with the topo is that it allows you to very quickly see the whole property and understand scale. Just walking a course can be problematic, especially if it's a complex site, as it's hard to understand it spatially. You can easily tie yourself in knots using this method alone, finding that holes don't quite fit together as seamlessly as they do when drawing from plan.

Tepetonka heat map

With all of this in place, my first step usually involves looking broadly at the property and trying to find areas that look interesting for golf, while at the same time starting to discount those pockets that are less suited. This could be because the ground is too flat or too steep, too close to a boundary, or maybe because the ground conditions are simply too challenging due to rock or swampland.

My eye is always drawn to interesting landforms. That might be a creek, a ravine, a coastline, some sand dunes, a high point of the property or just a beautifully contoured section of the site. Then I like to figure out how to squeeze as much golf into that interesting ground as possible. And ideally, I'll try to return to that point multiple times in the round.

Green sites and natural fairway corridors often stick out, and I'll draw any that look particularly interesting early on. Variety is key, so I'll always try to balance a good mixture of greens set up high, down low (such as if there is a natural punchbowl), plus using natural drop-offs to one side of the green or the other. Hole orientation and fairway contours are also important to vary, finding a mix of holes playing through natural valleys alongside those on top of a ridgeline or playing from peak to peak.

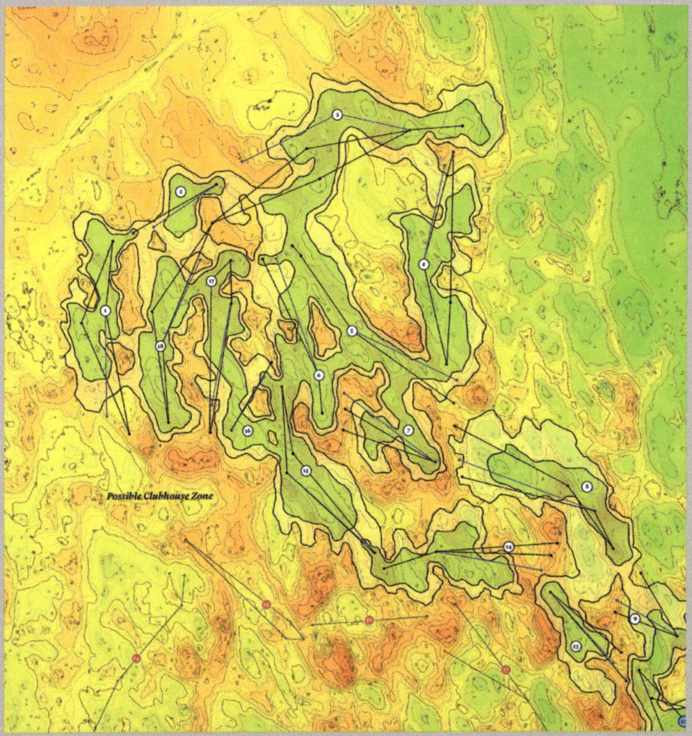

Developed routing for Tepetonka

Where a long feature allows for multiple holes to use the hazard – such as a barranca, creek or clifftop – it's important to vary the types of holes that play along it. A par-4 or par-5 playing along or just across the edge of the steep drop can be the making of some world-class architecture, but let's avoid playing four holes like it in a row. So when routing a course with such a dominant landform, I generally see if there can be multiple touchpoints through the round, and ideally holes are laid out so that some have the feature on the right, others on the left, some might use it as a backdrop or maybe even a couple play directly over it. Pebble Beach provides a great example of this. Holes 4 through 9 play with the coast along the right, including a few shots played directly over the cliffs, then the course turns inland before again coming back to the ocean with 17 played directly towards the water and the famous 18th skirting the edge of the cliffs, but this time the hazard is on the left of the hole.

We tried to achieve a similar thing at Arm End in Tasmania. The routing makes a neat figure eight to ensure we had a good mix of holes with the water on the left, as there were on the right, plus a few that use the ocean as a backdrop to the green site.

For me, the right mix is a combination of fieldwork and studying the topographic plan. My preference is to see the site and walk it early on, and then spend time on the topo plan, knowing generally what lies within and around the course. Then once we have a couple of routing options laid out, go back and spend a few days walking them. Typically, these will then get adjusted in the field but following that visit, we are usually in a position to settle on a design.

The nature of the site itself often dictates how many viable routing options exist. Undulating, expansive properties will have countless possibilities, while a small, flattish site may have just a few, with much of the challenge being spatial, and trying to make the holes fit, rather than laying out the holes based purely on the contours.

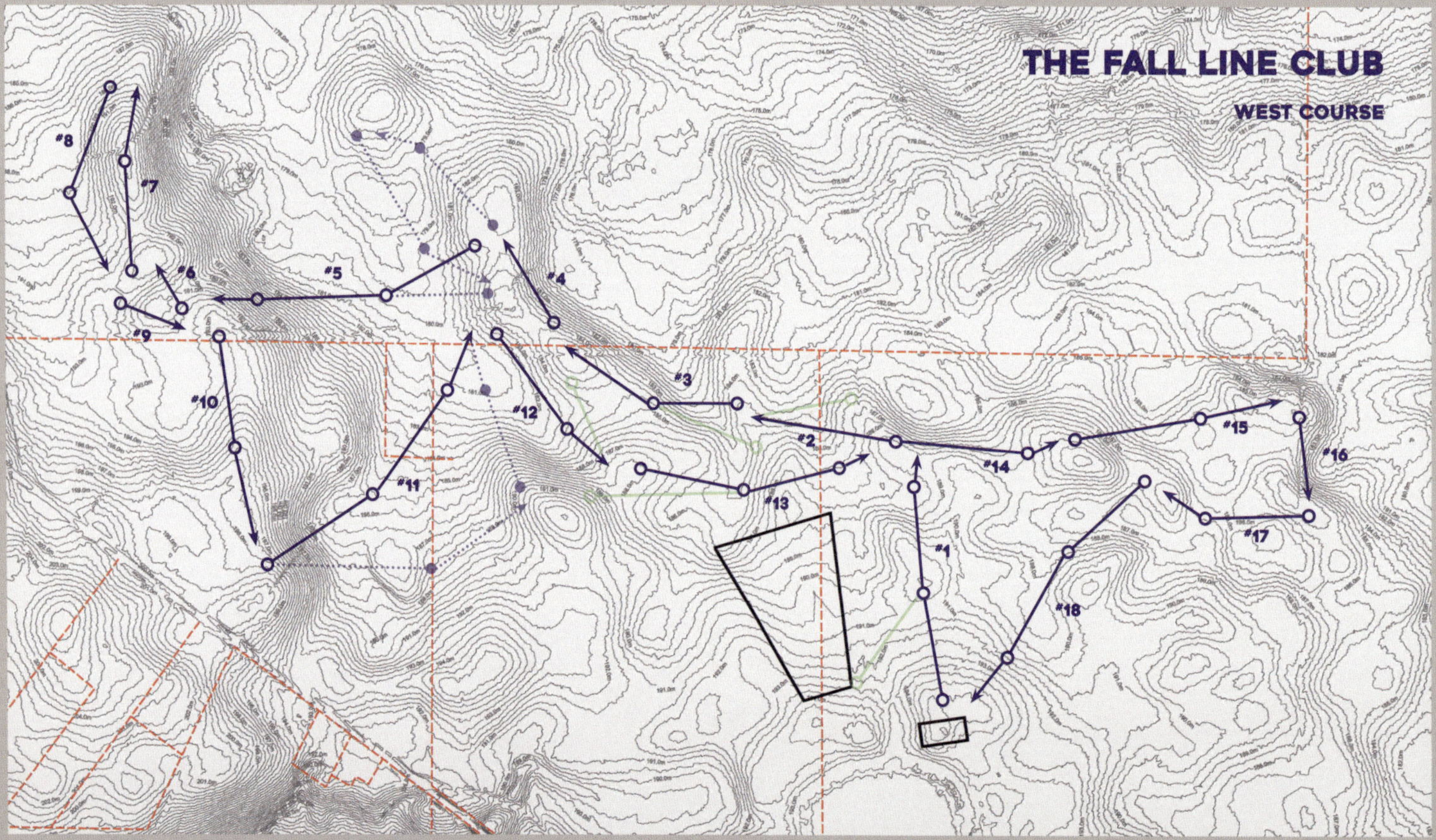

Contour map and initial routing for The Fall Line, Mauk, Georgia, United States

Clearing plan for The Fall Line

> 'One method that yields more interesting results is to start by grading the site, using topographic details from other interesting properties, to help create some good-looking golf ground, and only then route the course.'

Architects don't always get to pick and choose these sorts of sites, and quite often we find ourselves dealing with a flat site composed of just a few contour lines. On these sorts of properties, the architect may decide to add some contours. However, no matter how imaginative a designer may be, the randomness that nature can provide cannot be copied or created in an office, so adding a lot of contours comes with its challenges. What often happens in this case is that the holes are first laid out and then mounds and contours are added around these holes in a way that fits the architect's eye. This usually results in fairly conventional holes, some mounds that serve to frame the holes, and none of the quirks found in nature. One method that yields more interesting results is to start by grading the site, using topographic details from other interesting properties, to help create some good-looking golf ground, and only then route the course. This way, some of the more natural and random contours and golf holes are created. To some extent, this is how we have designed our new links course in Luling, Texas.

The Fall Line after initial clearing works

Practical Considerations

As the routing plan develops, a number of other practical factors need to be taken into consideration, starting with perhaps the most crucial early decision: the placement of the clubhouse.

Clubhouse

Many a routing has been compromised by a poorly chosen clubhouse site, which is why, wherever possible, we like to influence its position as part of the routing process. Running services (gas, electricity, sewer) and constructing roads is expensive, so developers often look to build the clubhouse close to the edge of the property. But what if the most interesting land is further into the property? If the aim is to link the holes back to the clubhouse and not have the course detached, as it is at Sand Hills in Nebraska, it will almost certainly mean the start and finish play over weaker parts of the property. This is the case on one of the famous links courses in the UK, where the clubhouse sits close to the street and the most interesting links land lies one or two holes further into the property.

Sometimes contours can also be a factor, as it was at Lake Karrinyup in Perth. The architect, Alex Russell, fought hard to build the clubhouse down low and by the lake to avoid steep hill climbing. The club opted to position the building high on a hill to take advantage of the views and late afternoon breeze – a pleasant relief in forty-degree summers. The only problem: it meant the 1st, 10th, 9th and 18th all had to negotiate the same hill. The 1st and 10th played down, while the 9th and 18th played up the steep rise.

The other clubhouse consideration concerns the number of holes. How many holes are there? Eighteen, thirty-six or more? In an ideal world, the club operates out of one main building and each course is within a short proximity to the clubhouse, so that golfers can easily walk between them to start and finish a round. This is how many of the older thirty-six-hole courses were laid out, such as at The Royal Melbourne, Winged Foot, Sunningdale and Medinah (fifty-four holes). But on many of the modern destination layouts, the dunes are so vast and spread out that this isn't possible without seriously compromising one or more of the layouts, and so the idea of smaller, satellite clubhouses to service the more remote courses evolved. Such is the case at Bandon Dunes and Sand Valley.

Avoiding the Sun

Avoiding a rising and setting sun should always be a consideration when laying out the holes. Generally, architects avoid an opening hole that plays due east and a finishing hole playing west.

Sometimes it's unavoidable, or avoiding the issue requires a significant change to the landscape or a compromised routing. For example, what if the dune-land naturally runs east–west, as it does at Barnbougle Dunes in Tasmania? With the dunes just wide enough for two holes, it was impossible to avoid a low sun at either the start or finish. Kingston Heath is another affected by the sun, although at this course it comes at the start of the round with the opening tee shot playing due-east – an added hazard to the already strong par-4 opener.

Returning Nines

In discussing returning nines, it's impossible not to recount Alister MacKenzie's famous quote from his 1933 book *The Spirit of St Andrews*:

'I believe I was the first to write articles emphasising the importance of the two loops of nine holes. During recent years in the United States I have had more sleepless nights owing to committees being obsessed by this principle than anything else, and I have often regretted that it had ever been propounded. If land for a golf course lends itself readily to constructing two loops, well and good, but it is a great mistake to sacrifice excellent natural features for the purpose of obtaining it.'

More often than not, returning nines as a design principle makes sense. At public courses, it allows more golfers to play the course each day, which increases revenue. And most members of private clubs also prefer the convenience of a two-tee start, if given a choice.

Sometimes, though, returning nines can be difficult. On coastal links land, for instance, which is often only a sliver of dunes just wide enough for two holes, out and back. Royal Dornoch, Royal Troon and The Old Course at St Andrews are just a few of the numerous examples where the turn is quite often the furthest point from the clubhouse.

At other times, returning nines limit the potential of the routing as you can only ever stray around four or five holes from the clubhouse. This is particularly common on expansive sites such as our Fall Line project in Georgia. Set on 1,500 acres, with some of the best land deep into the property, a returning nine would have seriously compromised the course had we not been able to venture nine or ten holes into the property before turning back.

View from the 16th tee at The Fall Line west after initial clearing

Cadence of the Course

The cadence of the course is another function of the routing and can add (or detract) from the round. Some architects opt to find the best group of holes and suggest that the numbers are what they are. Others may choose to manipulate the routing or a sequence of holes in order to play with the rhythm and flow of the course.

Is the aim to provide a friendly start and design the course to build in both drama and difficulty as the round progresses? Or does the architect prefer the course to start strong and 'separate the men from the boys' early on?

Cart Paths Versus Connectivity

Routing a course on a site that is to be primarily navigated by carts often requires less skill. Knowing that the golfers have the convenience of jumping in a cart to travel between holes allows the architect to simply find the best eighteen holes without the challenge of working out how they fit together. At some resorts, it's not uncommon to face a 200- or 300-metre drive between holes.

At most of my favourite courses, there is an elegant connection from one hole to the next, which gives the golfer a feeling they are on a journey rather than playing eighteen separate holes. Minimising the distance between holes helps to achieve this, as does linking green to tee using short grass, a technique we developed early in our careers on the Sandbelt, and have used on many projects around the world.

Roughing in the fairways at Tepetonka

'At most of my favourite courses, there is an elegant connection from one hole to the next, which gives the golfer a feeling they are on a journey.'

LEFT
The 6th green and 7th tee at Peninsula Kingswood, Victoria, Australia

Practice Facilities

Practice areas often fight for the same real estate as the golf course, with members enjoying the convenience of being able to walk to the driving range or pitching area. Depending on a number of factors, such as the clubhouse position, topography and the number of holes around the clubhouse, this might be a tough ask. Due to their size, a chipping or putting green is generally easy to locate, but a driving range, which can be as much as twenty acres, is a different story. We always caution against prioritising practice over the quality of the course, and quite often this means siting the range away from the clubhouse.

At the end of all this, you have a routing. A draft anyway ... and now the most difficult task is in front of you. A second routing! Figuring out a second option can be harder than you think. Being so invested in the first routing can make it difficult to look at the site another way, but the routing is the backbone of the design, and as the soul of the course, it's critical to explore every option. Then, like adding layers of clothing, the other elements are brought in. The contouring of the greens, the position of the tees and, finally, adding the jewellery with the detailing of the bunkers and some texture and detail to the roughs.

In flushing out the various routing options, some compromises will more than likely need to be made. Sometimes you have to give up your favourite holes because they may not represent the greater good or compromise a loop of holes elsewhere. But herein lies the challenge of routing a course: you can't keep all 118 holes.

LONDON HEATHLANDS
UNITED KINGDOM

WORDS AND PHOTOGRAPHY
BY WILLIAM WATT

LEFT
The 14th green and 15th tee at
The Addington, Surrey, England

On sandy soil encircling London lies the crucible of golf's golden age. Here, amidst heather and pine, Colt, MacKenzie and Simpson crafted the architectural principles that would define inland golf and shape course design for generations to come.

At Long Last

To be sitting on a plane destined for my favourite international hub, Singapore, and then onto one of my favourite cities, London, is both a relief and cause for excitement. I'll be staying with my best mate of nearly thirty years, which would have been reason enough for the trip back in the day. But I'll also be learning as much as I can about golf in the London Heathlands, or the Surrey Sandbelt, as some are calling it. The area has been (re)gaining prominence in recent years for its underappreciated architectural significance, an aspirational aesthetic and a truly historic collection of courses. Shoot days at Sunningdale, New Zealand and St George's Hill are on the agenda, and whatever else I can find time to explore. (Pleasingly, all three clubs were mentioned by Rory McIlroy just a few days earlier when asked about his best examples of the Heathland region).

Expectations of the Heathland courses are high, particularly given we are in late September, which should make for some beautiful conditions for both golf and photography. I've packed my Mamiya medium-format analogue camera, along with a generous amount of film, so I'm excited to give that a good run. I'm hoping to play a bit of golf as well, although a recent back injury means that's only a maybe. As we fly over Australia's Great Dividing Range and I look beyond it to the vast desert landscape of The Outback, I'm almost salivating for the lush rolling hills and pine forests of Surrey. As much as I love my home country, Australia is a big, brown, brawny beast of a place, and it can at times feel isolating. Every now and then, I have to get out and feed my eyes, and my camera lenses, on some more intricate, gentle and refined fodder.

RIGHT Golfers tee-off on the 2nd hole of The Old Course, Sunningdale.

Sunningdale

After a night in London to find my feet and try to convince myself that jet lag isn't a thing, I'm up at 5 am and on the road to Sunningdale. Having been told by a trusted golf friend that 'just to set foot on the property will be an experience', it would be fair to say I'm expecting something special. With thirty-six holes to explore and nothing else on the agenda, even a typically London morning of low cloud and light drizzle doesn't dampen my spirits. Pulling into the car park, I'm taken aback by something that should have been obvious prior to coming here but hadn't occurred to me: a palpable sense of history.

Most of my research before coming had been about finding a mix of courses that best exemplified the playing experience of the region. But walking alongside the historic clubhouse, with the silhouette of the massive club emblem oak tree towering over me, it's clear that's only part of the story. I'm standing at the epicentre of what is known as golf's first golden age – a period when those who would one day be considered the game's greatest architects gathered to create world-class golf away from the coast.

The London Heathlands sit atop the heathland belt, a ring of sandy, well-draining soil around London. This natural gift presented the perfect canvas to create compelling golf, and fortunately at the time (1890–1930), was not suitable for many other purposes. This period, in which most of the famous London Heathland courses were built, wasn't just the genesis of golf's golden age – it was a unique moment when greats like Colt, MacKenzie and Simpson regularly gathered, debated and refined their ideas.

Dr Alister MacKenzie's Thirteen Core Golf Course Design Principles

01. The course, where possible, should be arranged in two loops of nine holes.

02. There should be a large proportion of good two-shot holes and at least four one-shot holes.

03. There should be little walking between the greens and tees, and the course should be arranged so that in the first instance there is always a slight walk forwards from the green to the next tee; then the holes are sufficiently elastic to be lengthened in the future if necessary.

04. The greens and fairways should be sufficiently undulating, but there should be no hill climbing.

05. Every hole should be different in character.

06. There should be a minimum of blindness for the approach shots.

07. The course should have beautiful surroundings, and all the artificial features should have so natural an appearance that a stranger is unable to distinguish them from nature itself.

08. There should be a sufficient number of heroic carries from the tee, but the course should be arranged so that the weaker player with the loss of a stroke, or portion of a stroke, shall always have an alternate route.

09. There should be infinite variety in the strokes required to play the various holes; that is, interesting brassie shots, iron shots, pitch and run-up shots.

10. There should be a complete absence of the annoyance and irritation caused by the necessity of searching for lost balls.

11. The course should be so interesting that even the scratch man is constantly stimulated to improve his game in attempting shots he has hitherto been unable to play.

12. The course should so be arranged that the long handicap player or even the absolute beginner should be able to enjoy his round in spite of the fact that he is piling up a big score. In other words, the beginner should not be continually harassed by losing strokes from playing out of sand bunkers. The layout should be so arranged that he loses strokes because he is making wide detours to avoid hazards.

13. The course should be equally good during winter and summer, the texture of the greens and fairways should be perfect and the approaches should have the same consistency as the greens.

The overlap was, in some cases, almost complete. These architects' shared philosophies are best surmised in MacKenzie's famous thirteen design principles, a doctrine of golf architecture that covered everything from the naturalness of design to the importance of strategic bunkering. Up until this point, none of this thinking had really been distilled, ordered and written down. Golf had been largely confined to linksland, where courses mostly designed themselves. After all, the original bunkers were exactly that – shelters where grazing sheep could escape the worst of the weather. Green sites were chosen wherever they lay in the land, and course designers were primarily tasked with connecting the dots and mowing in some fairways (not that this is a bad thing!). But as golf moved inland, closer to large population centres like London and often onto heavily forested sites, the decision-making had to be sharpened. Who knows, maybe Harry Colt, Old Tom Morris, Willie Park Jnr or others before them came up with this all on their own with a flash of epiphany, and everyone else just copied their homework. But it is more likely the ideas emerged from a collective awakening and exchange of concepts. How many incidental conversations, connections and shared insights must have occurred during this period to create something that can now be remembered more than a hundred years later as a true 'golden age'? Oh, to be sat in one of those booths at the local taphouse, listening to the future of the game emerge.

View above the 15th on Sunningdale Old

But I digress! I haven't even walked into the clubhouse, let alone out onto the course, and Sunningdale has me daydreaming about clinking glasses with the greats. It's probably because, from an Australian perspective, I was always drawn to imagine MacKenzie's famous visit in 1926, which had a very different dynamic. In that instance, MacKenzie was already a renowned expert, espousing his great knowledge on the game, which was eagerly lapped up by local committees eager to improve their golf offering. I would picture him overlooking the current-day 6th green at The Royal Melbourne West, explaining his well-formulated philosophy to Alex Russell and greenskeeper Mick Morcom. But what happened in London fifteen or twenty years prior was really where those philosophies were forged. In part, right where I was standing, on the 1st tee of Sunningdale Old.

Designed by Scotsman Willie Park Jr, the original layout at Sunningdale is carved through some wonderful forested terrain. It set a new standard for inland golf when it opened in September 1901, demonstrating that courses away from the coast could be every bit as strategic and beautiful as their seaside counterparts. In many ways, it formed a blueprint for what inland golf could be. The large, undulating greens, inventive use of heathland plants both as hazards and aesthetic features, wide playing corridors and excellent hole variety across the routing means this course has stood up remarkably well over 120 years of golf evolution.

The stretch of holes from 3 through to 11 are a standout. Here, the thriving heather forms distinctive, coral-like outcrops along ridges, bumps and bunker edges, as well as across larger expanses such as tee carries and bordering fairways, offering pops of colour and rugged contrast to the perfectly manicured playing surfaces. The tee shot on the 3rd, as well as the heaving fairway and dramatic approach shot into the par-4 7th, are particular highlights. The tee shots on 10 and 11 are both glorious for opposite reasons – 10 entices you with a stunning view of a strategically bunkered, checkerboard fairway, bordered by stately pine trees and a quaint halfway house beyond the green. After a short stop for a bacon sandwich and coffee, the 11th asks you to hit blind over a hill of heather with only a white pole, and perhaps some encouragement from a caddie, to go by.

The 12th and 13th work towards and over a large ridge, before a flatter run of holes that are beautifully framed by pines, heather and imaginative bunkering. The run home is also a treat, with the 17th approach and green site occupying a particularly beautiful part of the property, especially when viewed with the historic clubhouse in the distance. The 18th green, towered over by that magnificent Oak tree, exudes history and charm.

The New course, Harry Colt's most significant contribution to the site in 1923 (he also 'tweaked' the Old Course during his time as Secretary), occupies the more adventurous and expansive south-eastern side of the property. While the 1st and 18th holes serve primarily as a direct route to and from the clubhouse, everything else on Colt's routing is grand and exciting. Somewhat surprisingly, Tom Simpson also had his say on the layout, having been called upon to redesign the 6th through 10th holes in 1934 to make the most of some more favourable land at the back of the 5th green. Five years later, Colt redesigned the new holes, reversing the loop that Simpson had created, and rebuilding several of his greens. Despite the complicated history of this part of the routing, it is a standout of current-day Sunningdale.Working out from the woods from the 4th, the elevated 5th tee provides a view of perhaps one of the best par-3s I have ever seen – mesmerising! Not to be outdone, the 6th tee reveals an expansive par-5 moving dramatically from left to right on terrain that suddenly feels exposed and raw. But it's not long until we are back in the forest, the 8th taking us back towards the 5th green. The holes through this stretch, from 9 to 12, run through the heart of the property and are incredibly atmospheric and tranquil. The par-4 13th brings us back out to the marshy land on the eastern edge of the property, where another beautiful par-3, the 14th, turns us around back towards the clubhouse. The 15th skilfully skirts this same boundary and features just the second water hazard on the property (the other being the 5th on the Old Course). With 16 and 17 offering significant elevation changes and wonderful shot-making, the slightly anticlimactic 18th can be more than forgiven – by this stage in the round, you are already trying to process the adventurous path you've just been on.

Tee view of the par-3 8th, Sunningdale Old

Sunningdale's refined, historic clubhouse

'It set a new standard for inland golf when it opened in September 1901, demonstrating that courses away from the coast could be every bit as strategic and beautiful as their counterparts.'

The rugged natural beauty of the heathland setting, unobscured by linear mowing lines

As my first true Harry Colt experience, for whatever reason, I had been expecting something quite stiff and refined. Perhaps it was the pronounced Englishness of both the man and the setting. But what I found at every turn was fun, imaginative golf. The overall aesthetic was also surprising – while the heather, sandy blowouts, rugged bunkering and roughly carved canals were distinctive and natural, this was contrasted with the stiff grandeur of the pine forests, the precision of manicured squared tee boxes and the striped-up fairways. As I would find out during the rest of my trip, squared-off tee boxes and bold lawn striping are standard fare around the London area, the only explanation for which I received was, 'That's just how we do it here.'

Coming from the Melbourne Sandbelt, where such agronomic practices would cause a superintendent to be laughed out of town (or at least taken aside for a quiet word), I found these showy mowing lines competed for attention with the natural elements. It felt like James Bond ordering a martini, but instead of specifying it to be 'shaken not stirred', insisting on a colourful paper umbrella. From a photography standpoint, at least, it created a compelling contrast and great fodder for my lens. But I do wonder if a significant club was brave enough to allow the conditioning to take on a more subtle and complementary role to the natural heathland setting, others might not soon follow suit.

But these arguments are merely a side note to what is a remarkable golf experience. Just as The Old Course at St Andrews manages to somehow distil the essence of links golf into eighteen holes, Sunningdale does the same for inland golf across its thirty-six.

The par-5 6th hole on The New Course at Sunningdale ventures into unfamiliar terrain. Seen from the tee, the green (top-right of frame) seems impossibly far away.

The 10th hole of The Old Course at Sunningdale leaves an indelible impression.

The iconic approach view of the 17th hole of The Old Course at Sunningdale

'Just as The Old Course at St Andrews manages to somehow distil the essence of links golf into eighteen holes, Sunningdale does the same for inland golf across its thirty-six.'

The donut bunker separates the 7th and 13th greens at New Zealand Golf Club.

New Zealand Golf Club and Hankley Common

The next morning brings another early start, and the prospect of a completely different golf experience at New Zealand Golf Club. Home to just 300 members, this is the sort of place where the history is palpable and exudes a certain mystique. The locker room features an unusual tradition – members' names are hand-painted onto the black wooden panels of their locker door. After passing, names are ceremoniously crossed out but left intact – even Sir Arthur Conan Doyle did not escape this fate.

My first question, as a part-Kiwi, was about the name of the club. I was directed to a framed explanation, which is understandable, given the complexity (and current-day sensitivity) of the answer. The short version is that the land the course sits on, originally part of the Royal Forest of Windsor, was named 'New Zealand' in the 1850s by owner Peter John Locke King in honour of his family's ties to the colony of the same name. His relative, Captain Henry King RN, had served as Resident Magistrate in New Zealand's Taranaki region (his original estate in New Plymouth, Brooklands, survives to this day as a public park).

'The green site on the distinctive 17th hole is a particularly beautiful spot, and I find myself soaking in this slice of pure heathland golf, watching members roll through at a pace that would make most clubs envious.'

The light London drizzle as I explore the course only enhances the tranquillity; the thick woods create an almost eerie silence broken only by the occasional tap of a woodpecker (the club's fitting emblem). Having played most of Melbourne's Sandbelt courses, there's something of Frankston Golf Club's privacy and atmosphere here, combined with Kingston Heath's topography and sophisticated design elements. Despite significant clearing works completed during recent years by Clayton, DeVries & Pont (CDP Golf), which has opened up the course, especially on the far paddock, it's clearly an ongoing battle to fight back the forest.

The sun finally breaks through after an hour or so, throwing long shadows across the fairways and greens. The eeriness recedes as the course lights up. The green site on the distinctive 17th hole is a particularly beautiful spot, and I find myself soaking in this slice of pure heathland golf, watching members roll through at a pace that would make most clubs envious. It's my first look at a Tom Simpson course, and my suspicion that he is a somewhat unheralded golden age architect is confirmed. There's deception, strategy and imagination throughout, and even within the par-68, there is enough variety to make this one of the great walks of the region.

BELOW
London drizzle adds to the atmosphere at New Zealand Golf Club.

The par-3 7th at Hankley Common

After an excellent pub meal, let down only by an undrinkable, room-temperature beer, the next stop of the day creates perhaps the greatest contrast of the trip.

Upon arrival at Hankley Common, it's clear the clubhouse doesn't have the historic atmosphere of my previous two experiences (although, to be fair, few do). When I arrive at the 1st tee, complete with its flower beds and artificial turf steps, I wonder if I've made the right choice driving the extra forty-five minutes from the city. All that changes when I crest the 1st fairway and see the green site. The way it sits in the land, with enticing contours leading down into the green, it's clear I'm about to experience something special.

While James Braid laid out the original nine holes in 1897, it was Harry Colt's expansion to eighteen holes in the 1920s that truly established Hankley's character. The par-3 2nd and par-4 3rd strengthen this belief – the green for the 3rd in particular makes running in a low approach irresistible, so beautiful are the contours and conditioning. I later learn the former superintendent from Morfontaine is now here, and his expertise shows in every closely mown surface.

After the somewhat incongruous 4th (apparently due to go under the knife soon), the routing really hits its straps. The 5th has a lovely green site, alongside the 8th, and the long uphill par-5 6th, bordered by marshy heathland, feels open and spacious – a welcome change from the previous heavily forested courses of yesterday and this morning. The par-3 7th is a wonderful one-shotter across a gully, offering panoramic views across the course and the entire region. Standing on the tee, you could easily imagine yourself in the Scottish Highlands. It's no surprise that the spectacular closing scenes of *Skyfall* (one of the best Bond films ever) were filmed just over the hill.

Hankley's heather areas are some of the healthiest and densest I've seen (word is that other Surrey clubs routinely visit an area nearby to harvest heather for their own courses). The integration of heather into the bunker complexes is notable, especially on the par-5 8th, where the bunker lips effectively bridge between fairway and vast expanses of purple-tinged rough, creating a uniquely appealing aesthetic.

The back nine starts in similarly open, exposed terrain, with slightly more gentle land movement. But from the 13th onwards, we could almost be back at Sunningdale, such is the similarity of forested backdrops and imaginative holes. The feeling of intimacy and warmth in this stretch adds a welcome contrast to the golf experience – I'm a sucker for a routing that offers distinct settings throughout the round. The occasional crack of gunfire from nearby military training grounds only adds to the wild atmosphere.

Hankley Common might not currently feature on many overseas visitors' must-play lists, but it absolutely should. This is a course that showcases heathland golf at its purest and most natural, and unlike most of its Surrey brethren, it will also encourage you to open your shoulders a little as you take in the open terrain.

The shapely 3rd green at Hankley Common

The par-4 10th at Hankley Common

The 8th tee at Hankley Common

'The occasional crack of gunfire from nearby military training grounds only adds to the wild atmosphere. Hankley Common might not currently feature on many overseas visitors' must-play lists, but it absolutely should.'

St George's Hill and The Addington

My final day in the region starts at St George's Hill, a club that impresses in layers. The approach through a private estate lined with grand country houses sets the tone – glimpses down gravel driveways reveal G-wagons, supercars, perfectly manicured topiary and very heavy front doors. The clubhouse itself resembles a castle and feels just as fortified. Used as a military hospital during World War I, its historic hallways are etched with names and dates, and there's a sense of permanence that's hard to ignore.

While most heathland courses in the region occupy gently rolling land, here the elevation changes are dramatic, creating a routing full of memorable moments. Today, the club maintains twenty-seven of Harry Colt's original thirty-six holes across three nines – known as the Red, Blue and Green courses – with the championship layout comprising the Red and Blue. I'm particularly keen to see the famous par-3 8th prior to restoration by some key members of the Renaissance Golf team. If the restoration can get it close to the pictures I have seen, it will once again be regarded as one of the world's great par-3s.

Photography proved challenging, despite a beautiful clear morning, with the dense forest of birch and pine trees casting blocked shadows across fairways and greens. With most holes facing west, a morning shoot was a rookie error. Maybe that jet lag was finally kicking in. But even with these limitations, the quality of the course and setting shone through. As I departed for my afternoon's destination at The Addington, it was exciting to think what the restoration at St George's Hill could bring.

I heard The Addington dubbed 'Sunningdale before Sunningdale', which succinctly tells you a bit about its standing in London golf circles, both then and now. But what makes this place special isn't just its history, but that it somehow managed to bring together two powerhouse schools of golf design from the golden era of golf architecture. The two schools were somewhat fluid, but primarily consisted of Fowler–Simpson–Abercromby on one side and Colt–MacKenzie–Alison on the other. The Addington is possibly the only place where these two worlds collided and, in doing so, created something spectacular.

JF 'Aber' Abercromby was a member at Huntercombe in 1901, Willie Park Jr's new course. Before long, he was doing design work at Worplesdon and Coombe Hill (with Park keeping an eye on things). When it came time to tackle The Addington in 1914, though, Park was overseas, so he turned to Harry Colt for counsel. It turned out to be a masterstroke. Some of the holes here must surely give modern architects pangs of jealousy at the audacity of the design, the kind that would never get approved today. And that's exactly what makes them brilliant.

The Addington's recent history is a cautionary tale. Previous owners meant well in aiming to preserve a classic piece of golf design heritage, but in refusing to change anything, including the (ever-growing) trees, the fairways were eventually about as wide as your average suburban driveway. All that strategic width that Aber and Colt had worked so hard to create? Gone.

Under new ownership by the Noades family, particularly Ryan Noades, who's properly obsessed with the place's history, Clayton, DeVries & Pont (CDP Golf) has been brought in and the restoration is about three-quarters done. CDP has gone deep – more than 200 pages of research deep – to deliver a faithful restoration. Once complete, it promises to be well and truly back on the map of London golf. The city views are spectacular – 'Aim at The Shard' has become a legitimate strategy on some holes. As the restoration has peeled back the layers, you can really see what made this place so special; it's like finding an old master painting under years of varnish.

After weaving back to north London through the endless maze of city streets, there's time to reflect on the heathlands with my host, Aussie-turned-Londoner Sam. It's clear that while I've hit some of the highlights, there's so much more to see and play. As a partner at a London architecture firm, Sam makes it clear that golf still has a role to play in business life in the city, as it likely always has. In the name of networking, he is forced to dine at the smorgasbord of excellent golf courses almost every other week. After a few years of this, he has barely repeated a round, such is the depth on offer.

As the weekend draws near, I'm tempted to chase another hit of London Heathland action, but the dreary London weather, along with a lunch invite to Sam's swanky local, makes up my mind. I've seen enough to form a strong impression, and with another good friend flying in from Norway for the weekend, it's time to embrace the moment and hang up the camera strap. For now.

The wild terrain of the par-5 16th at The Addington

'Aim for The Shard' on the 14th at The Addington

Distinctive rocky outcrops dot the approach to the 12th at Fontainebleau.

Fontainebleau

A hand-painted sign reading simply *GOLF* marks the entrance to one of France's most intriguing courses. It's a fitting introduction to Fontainebleau, where understatement and history combine to create something magical. Just forty-five minutes by train from Paris, Fontainebleau has long served as a refuge for those seeking to escape from the capital. Napoleon himself preferred its palace to Versailles, though sadly there's no record of him ever picking up a mashie. The town itself is gorgeous – a vibrant university hub that has grown up around one of France's most spectacular châteaux.

The gravel driveway winds through an ancient forest before revealing a clubhouse that looks like it was lifted straight from a Wes Anderson film. Inside, a remarkable century-old fresco by artist and former member Paul Tavernier wraps around the walls, depicting various golf scenes. The emerald green carpet, matching walls and staff uniforms create an almost impossibly cool atmosphere that's very French.

Tom Simpson, who designed much of his best work in France during the 1920s and 1930s, found himself with an interesting challenge here. The site offers remarkable natural features, including dramatic rocky outcrops, but also contains relatively flat sections that required his creative touch. His solution was to use a prominent rocky hill as a dramatic focal point – the routing revisits it several times throughout the round, each time revealing a different perspective.

The clubhouse dining room that looks out over the 1st tee

The opening tee shot, played away from the clubhouse dining room with this hill as backdrop, immediately presents the golfer with Simpson's bold hazard style. A string of bunkers stretches right across the fairway, demanding both accuracy and careful strategy. As I watch a group tee-off, the first player sprays his shot into the trees right of the fairway. He looks back at his playing partners, perplexed, and simply asks, 'Ça *va*?'. This brevity and ease perfectly sum up the relaxed French golf scene for me.

This forceful use of cross-hazards appears throughout the round – Simpson was clearly not afraid to demand something from the golfer here. It's a contrast to his work in the UK, where he often let the natural contours do more of the defensive work. However, his use of camouflage bunkering is evident on the 12th fairway – looking back from the green, hazards that caught the eye from the tee completely disappear, blending seamlessly into the landscape.

Some of the driving lines feel a touch restrictive today, particularly on holes like the 13th. The bunkers could use some additional shaping too – they're well placed but lack the drama of Simpson's original vision. The course would benefit from selective tree removal (although that could be difficult in some cases, given some date from the 1500s!), and further reintroduction of heather to bring it closer to its original design. Fortunately, that's exactly what CDP Golf plans to do in the coming years.

While I'm excited to see those design updates, I hope nothing else about this place changes. Places that exude this sort of character and flair are rare, and are part of what makes golf such a culturally rich and beautiful game to explore.

LEFT Trees planted by King Henry IV in the 15th century can be found across the property.

TOM SIMPSON: THE FORGOTTEN ARCHITECT

WORDS BY MIKE CLAYTON
FEATURING QUOTES FROM TOM SIMPSON
PHOTOGRAPHY BY WILLIAM WATT

'To associate an art of the dignity of Architecture with so humble a pursuit as golf may appear at first glance to be a little incongruous.'

The 16th green at Tom Simpson's New Zealand Golf Club

RIGHT Above Simpson's par-3 10th at New Zealand Golf Club

In the summer of 1980, as part of an Australian team with Tony Gresham, John Kelly and Roger Mackay, I made my first trip to the European continent to play the French Amateur Championship at Chantilly. It was a time when no one spoke much about golf architecture, no one was writing any notable books (or even magazine articles) on the subject and we assumed the best courses in the world were the ones we saw the pros playing on the tour in the United States. There was, of course, no accounting for our ignorance.

Unsurprisingly, none of us had heard of Tom Simpson. We left Paris enamoured with his courses, but none the wiser about the man who made them. Not even after playing a match the day after the final against a French team at Morfontaine did we enquire as to who had designed them. Even worse, we headed to Royal Porthcawl for the British Amateur a couple of weeks later and again failed to make the Simpson connection or come away with any understanding of his immense contribution to golf architecture.

Simpson's Chantilly is a wonderful course, and in 1988, 1989 and 1990, it hosted the French Open, before the architecturally unfathomable decision to move the tournament to a purpose-built 'championship course' not far away. It was the old making way for the new. One wonders what Simpson would have made of it all. Donald Steel, in his foreword to Fred Hawtree's biography of Simpson, perfectly captured the architect's provocative nature: 'It is a fair deduction that his tendency for going out on a limb meant his views were more likely to be heard. In today's technological age, Facebook and Twitter would have been tailor-made for him.

'Never once in my forty years' experience has a great player, amateur or professional – John Low excepted – offered me anything but the worst possible advice. I am forced to regard the good player, amateur and professional, as an outstanding menace to the game on what constitutes a good hole.'

'The 17th hole at St Andrews is one of the finest, if not the finest, golfing holes in the world. It causes mental effort to be at a premium and physical effort to be at a discount.'

'Blow it up. I don't think there are many worse holes in world golf.' Robert McIntyre (Dunhill Links 2024)

Simpson's Background and Philosophy

Born into prosperity, Simpson chose golf course architecture at a time when the profession was transitioning from an era where courses were predominantly laid out by golf professionals. As Alister MacKenzie had abandoned medicine for golf design, Simpson left behind the confines of a London law office for a more adventurous calling. The two men understood more interesting courses would popularise the game and MacKenzie, ever the doctor, noted that his former patients, after taking up the game, were rarely seen in his surgery again.

'Golf can claim without exception to be the most flexible game in the world, almost as flexible and self-adapting as the British Constitution. It differs from the majority of games in not having the ground mapped out with a precise regularity. There are no lines or circles to denote areas of play.'

Simpson's financial independence allowed him to speak his mind freely, particularly when it came to golf club committees. As Steel notes, 'A golf course architect who intends to indulge in a little mischievous teasing of golf club green committees will feel much more frisky with that sort of insurance at the bank.' Simpson himself was delightfully direct on the subject, describing as 'abominations' almost half the original greens at Ireland's County Louth; this is but one example of his fearless dispensing of advice to a committee.

'When a member finds himself on the Green Committee, he feels it up to him to function and to justify his election. That is when the trouble begins.'

The uphill par-3 3rd at New Zealand Golf Club

The French Connection

Our first day at Morfontaine introduced me to a magnificent, tranquil place with its main eighteen; the wild, short, nine-hole Valliere course; and a beautiful, perfectly scaled stone clubhouse. During the weeks of those long-ago Chantilly Opens, I'd head over at least once to play at Simpson's architectural masterclass. And, for a club with a reputation as one of the hardest to open gates in golf, they couldn't have been more welcoming.

For me, Simpson's Morfontaine is akin to Seve Ballesteros's driving. The great man wasn't the best driver in the game (Greg Norman hit just as far and generally straighter), but he hit the best drives – low rips through a facing wind, high, soaring bombs (in the modern parlance) to take advantage of it when it was behind and big, impressive shapes best suited to the question the hole was asking.

Morfontaine may not be the world's best course but there are few better places to play golf. Its quiet, understated solitude offers something increasingly rare: a pure golf experience unmarred by the consequences of a land developer fixated on using golf to sell real estate, or the modern obsession with 'championship' courses. Simpson, working in a more enlightened era, understood a golf course deemed too short to hold professional tournaments could nonetheless be a serious course.

'The great statesmanlike courses, such is one's feeling, should only be played by the heroes. The incompetent generation might well be advised to leave them alone. They are simply tempted to their destruction.'

Simpson understood something that modern golf has largely forgotten: there's room for both championship tests and courses built for the game most people play. His New Zealand Golf Club near London remains one of the finest examples of this philosophy – a par-68 layout stretching to barely 6,000 yards remains one of the game's most admired courses. As Ran Morrissett, who heads the world top-100 course panel, observes, there's much to celebrate about a 6,000-yard course where you use all fourteen clubs and shake hands on the 18th green in three hours.

The rolling fairways of Fontainebleau

The par-3 10th at Golf de Fontainebleau

This approach wasn't unique to Simpson. Along with his contemporaries Harry Colt, Alister MacKenzie, Herbert Fowler and JF Abercromby, he sought to move golf architecture beyond the purely penal style that had dominated the game's early years. Their mission was to develop courses that would both challenge and charm players of all abilities – a stark contrast to the previous era's fixation with punishing every poor shot.

'The vital thing about a hole is that it must either be more difficult than it looks or look more difficult than it is. It must never look what it is.'

While Harry Colt was crafting masterpieces across The Netherlands at De Pan, Eindhoven and The Hague, Simpson focused his attention on France. His portfolio there includes many of the country's finest courses: Chantilly, Morfontaine, Fontainebleau, Hardelot and Chiberta near Biarritz. Each showcases his ability to work with the natural landscape, much like Abercromby achieved with his classics at The Addington (one sadly lost to London housing after World War II).

Simpson's work in France was often commissioned by the era's elite. As Steel notes, he 'seemed to enjoy a monopoly in designing courses for eminent people on their private estates, something quite fashionable for a period between the two wars.' His clients included Lord Louis Mountbatten, Sir Philip Sassoon (a politician and son of Aline de Rothschild) and the Duc de Gramont (whose title dated back to 1648). At Chantilly, Baron Édouard de Rothschild was instrumental in both the formation and financing of the club.

Meanwhile, Alister MacKenzie took the concepts of strategic design to far-flung corners of the globe including Argentina, New Zealand and Australia, where he was commissioned – after Colt had declined the club's offer – to make a new course for the members at The Royal Melbourne. As Simpson had shown the French what great golf looked like, so did Colt in both England and The Netherlands, and MacKenzie in far-away Australia.

Design Principles and Legacy

'Many of the things that contribute to a great course are not always appreciated at their full value; criticisms are often directed against the very features to which much of their greatness is due.'

Simpson and his contemporaries understood that their influence would extend beyond their built works, and that they needed to document their philosophies for future generations. A remarkable quartet of books emerged: MacKenzie followed his 1920 work *Golf Architecture* with *The Spirit of St Andrews* in the early 1930s; his American partner, Robert Hunter, produced *The Links*; George Thomas wrote *Golf Architecture in America*; and Simpson, collaborating with H N Wethered, gave us *The Architectural Side of Golf*. These books, which have become the sacred texts of golf course architecture, grow more relevant with each passing decade. Like the courses their authors created, their ideas have found new resonance with modern audiences, who recognise their timeless wisdom and the brilliance of their work.

The 9th hole approach at Fontainebleau

A look back up the 9th at New Zealand Golf Club

This appreciation wasn't immediate. In the decades following World War II – when modernist design philosophies emerged – these classical, underappreciated principles fell from favour. It took the perspective of time for the golf world to properly evaluate Simpson and his contemporaries. Now, contrasted against the work of post-war architects, their timeless principles and naturalistic approach appear more brilliant than ever.

'All good courses laid out in recent times owe their success to the fact that the architect sought inspiration from the old, classic courses, in particular St Andrews. The further back in time we seek our inspiration the more successful the course.'

Time has more than vindicated the work of Simpson and his contemporaries. Indeed, the current renaissance in golf course architecture – which began with Coore and Crenshaw's remarkable Sand Hills in Nebraska – draws direct inspiration from the golden age. Today's finest architects create courses that would feel familiar to Simpson, a testament to the enduring brilliance of his principles.

'It is only the mad masterpieces of the world that live in one's memory, such as holes 12, 13, 14, 16 and 17 at St Andrews, Sea Headrig at Prestwick, the 4th at Woking, the 14th at Liphook, the 13th at West Sussex and the 8th (now the 12th) at Addington, to mention a few of the classics.'

Because Simpson confined his work primarily to Europe, his name may not resonate as widely as some of his contemporaries who ventured to America's shores. But to walk the fairways at Fontainebleau or New Zealand Golf Club – where strategy, beauty and playability combine in perfect harmony – is to experience golf architecture at its finest. His courses, like his writings, remind us that the principles of great golf design are timeless, and true artistic genius needs no translation.

The par-3 7th at Fontainebleau

ST GEORGE'S HILL: HARRY COLT'S HIDDEN MASTERPIECE

SURREY, ENGLAND

WORDS BY JASPER MINERS
PHOTOGRAPHY BY WILLIAM WATT

LEFT
The beautiful opening par-4 at St George's Hill

St George's Hill Golf Club opened in October 1913. Several months later, after the start of World War I in July 1914, St George's iconic clubhouse was turned into a military hospital. The club's origin story is fascinating – property developer Mr Tarrant had initially proposed an unusual scheme, where each of eighteen property buyers would design one hole of the golf course. Fortunately, a local greenkeeper steered him towards Harry Colt instead.

What followed was a golf architect's dream commission: Colt was given both an unlimited budget and complete creative freedom, unencumbered by meddling committees for demanding owners. The result was so impressive that Colt himself declared it 'a rattling fine thing, perhaps the best in London.' Coming from a man who considered Swinley Forest his favourite creation, this was high praise indeed.

The Layout

Colt's masterful routing at St George's Hill takes the form of a figure-eight, with both nines returning to the clubhouse. In a brilliant piece of design efficiency, the 9th and 18th greens share a single putting surface, while the 1st and 10th tees spring from common ground – all four elements cascading dramatically down the hillside before the clubhouse.

That clubhouse, one of golf's most iconic structures, has its own remarkable story. Originally conceived as a Canadian log cabin, it was instead built of brick and mortar with a thatched roof. When fire gutted the building's interior and roof in the early 1920s, the outer walls survived – leading to today's architectural gem, albeit not quite as first envisioned.

The course itself has evolved over time. While today's world-class layout comprises the Red and Blue nines, there was once much more. Between 1929 and 1939, Colt added another eighteen holes at Weybridge. He designed the original eighteen to be 'long and tigerish,' while the second eighteen was crafted to be 'short and cunning.' While many holes of this second course have been reclaimed by nature, beneath the overgrowth, their architectural features remain intact. The current nine-hole Green course occupies roughly ten of these original holes, with the others waiting silently for rediscovery.

Strategic Design

Adding to the property's architectural richness is a forgotten gem: a third 18-hole Colt creation in the form of a putting course near the clubhouse, left of the 9th green and 1st tee. Only one other such Colt putting course has been documented, laid out a few years earlier at nearby Stoke Park.

But it's the downhill par-3 8th that best showcases Colt's genius. Here, the tee shot carries a valley to reach a dramatic two-tiered green perched on the opposite ridge. The hole's features read like poetry: the 'Chasm Bunker' tears between the green's upper and lower tiers, while the 'Pits of Penance' – a series of bunkers carved into the facing valley wall – create an intimidating backdrop from the tee.

The green itself is a masterpiece of strategic design. While severely tilted from back to front, Colt incorporated an ingenious 'bathtub' feature between the two tiers. This subtle depression serves dual purposes: it provides a pathway between otherwise disconnected levels and, if played cleverly, can be used to slingshot approaches towards certain pin positions. This same brilliant feature appears again on the combined 9th and 18th greens, highlighting Colt's consistency in strategic thinking.

The layers of complexity at St George's Hill reveal themselves slowly, like chapters in a masterwork. This was Colt at the height of his powers, so confident in his innovative design that he brought photographs of his work to show George Crump at Pine Valley in 1913 – evidence of what was considered avant-garde in pre-war London.

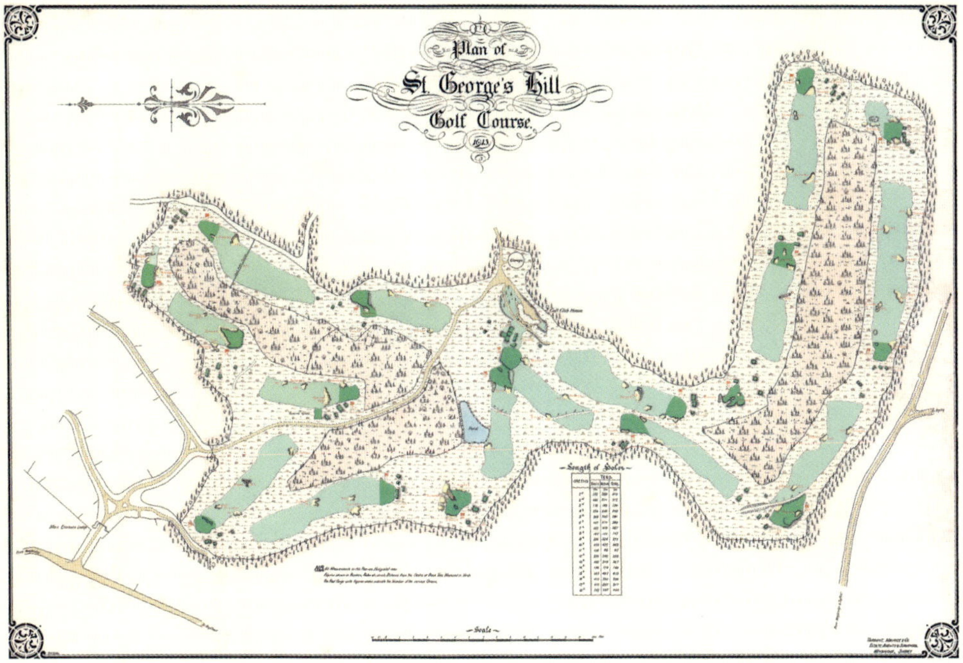

A Legacy Revealed

What makes St George's Hill truly exceptional is the purity of Colt's vision. Here was a rare instance where he not only had complete creative freedom but personally oversaw construction. More significantly, it stands as possibly the world's only thirty-six-hole venue featuring Colt's undiluted work. Even Sunningdale, often cited in this category, can't make this claim – Colt himself insisted on crediting Willie Park Jr for the Old Course when others tried to attribute it to him.

While many celebrate St George's Hill as a world-class eighteen-hole course with an iconic clubhouse, its true significance may lie in what's yet to come. The property stands on the precipice of becoming perhaps the most important golf course restoration project in the world. Beyond preserving Colt's legacy, a proper restoration would showcase his work at its absolute peak – not just in the overall design but in individual holes like the masterful 8th, 10th and 17th.

Already regarded as one of the world's eminent heathland golf courses, St George's Hill could, with a bold embrace of Colt's original vision, stake a claim as the very best of its kind.

LEFT Bill Waugh's painting of the par-3 8th, hopefully soon to be reinstated

SAND HILLS NEBRASKA, USA

WORDS AND PHOTOGRAPHY
BY LUKAS MICHEL

In remote Nebraska, amid endless prairieland, a revolution began. Sand Hills wasn't just a counterpoint to cookie-cutter developments – it rekindled golf's soul. From this minimalist masterpiece emerged a design renaissance that would inspire Bandon Dunes, Barnbougle and a return to golf's classical principles worldwide.

The late 1980s saw America's economy booming, driving unprecedented demand for housing. Suburbs were often expanding to less naturally inviting regions on the outskirts of cities, and developers were looking for ways to make these communities more attractive. Golf courses had long been recognised for their natural beauty, and golf and residential developments weren't a new concept. In fact, many of the world's best courses intermingle with homes – Pebble Beach, Pinehurst and Sunningdale. Property developers saw this proven concept and ran with it, resulting in a huge demand for golf architects, which was so great that it outstripped their ability to supply. To fulfil demand, their methods of design and construction became streamlined to a production-line approach. Often hemmed in by pre-planned housing on unattractive sites, the golfing corridors would be defined by the developers and left to the golf architect to rough in a hole design before sending off the plans to a contractor to build the work – sometimes without the architect even visiting the site.

The sport had been in a healthy position for the preceding thirty or so years, with charismatic superstars like Arnold Palmer, Gary Player, Jack Nicklaus, Seve Ballesteros and Greg Norman passing the torch from one generation to the next and keeping the sport popular among the masses. With participation numbers growing, golf course owners became less discerning of quality design. Tee times and memberships were selling fast, so what was the problem? By all the metrics at the time, golf and the golf architecture business were booming. But metrics by definition are a measure of quantities, and often miss the other side of the coin: quality. With the obsession for more and more golf courses, the quality of these modern designs took a hit. Architects were unable to spend valuable time onsite, extracting nuanced design features from the land or massaging these features into a design where sites were inspiring. Consequently, courses were poorly routed, constructed with tactless mounding and bunkering, and created with little thought-provoking strategy.

Enter Richard 'Dick' Youngscap. By profession, Youngscap was a building architect, but by passion, he was a golfer. Youngscap's first taste of golf course development was with the late Pete Dye at Firethorn, a manufactured links in Lincoln, Nebraska. Why manufacture linksland, though, when the real deal is a few hundred miles down the road? Youngscap certainly wasn't the first golfer inspired by the rolling prairieland of central Nebraska, known officially as the Sand Hills. Hundreds of people would put their hand up to say that they had the idea to build a golf course on that tumbling sandy soil, which closely resembles the boldest linksland of the British Isles. Youngscap certainly wasn't the last to have that idea either, based on the courses that have emerged recently, including Dismal River, the Prairie Club, Wild Horse and Ballyneal. What Youngscap had was the gumption and, as many would let him know, stupidity to actually try to build a course in one of the most desolate areas of North America. After passingly making a comment to one of the land brokers in the area to let him know of any properties that come to market, Youngscap was fortunately contacted a short time later regarding a parcel of 8,100 acres. Small by the standard of other properties in the area, Youngscap's parcel was still big enough to accommodate probably fifty golf courses. Youngscap would understand quite quickly, however, that in this remote area, where the nearest town of Mullen had a population of just a few hundred people, the local residents could only support the operation of a single golf course.

With a fantastic property, it was now down to selecting an architect who could make the golf worthy of the land. Based on their previous relationship, it seemed obvious that Pete Dye would be the first in line for the project, but it was Bill Coore and Ben Crenshaw who secured it. A serendipitous series of relationships and events connected the three. Legendary course superintendent Doug Petersan, who at the time was at Prairie Dunes, had worked with Coore and Crenshaw on some architectural tweaks at the significant Kansas course. Simultaneously, Youngscap was having maintenance issues with his Lincoln golf course, Firethorn, firing the superintendent, promoting his young assistant and, based on his reputation and recommendations, engaging Doug Petersan to be a mentor. Thus, it was Petersan who introduced the three significant figures of Sand Hills to each other, fostering one of the most important relationships in modern golf.

When Ben Crenshaw first stepped foot on site in the Sand Hills in September 1990, it wasn't the first time he'd laid eyes on the land. Ben had been inspired by an article that appeared in *National Geographic* magazine in October 1978. 'Land of Long Sunsets' by John Madsen wrote largely of the area's ranching, but importantly included photographs showcasing the landscape. These photographs immediately took Crenshaw's attention, and had stuck with him. For Coore, the feeling was similar. On a walk around Prairie Dunes with Doug Petersan years earlier, Coore mentioned the quality of the land there. Petersan stopped and turned. 'I know where there's land even better than this – the Sand Hills of Nebraska'. And so, with their own lofty expectations, as well as Youngscap's and the numerous others who had spoken about the place, Coore and Crenshaw set out on numerous site visits in the next two years to establish a routing.

Obviously, not all the land was appropriate, based on various geographical constraints, but the pair was able to whittle down the 8,100 acres to a much smaller parcel in a valley beyond a ridgeline near the Dismal River (where the clubhouse was to be located). Through the routing process, the pair famously laid out over 130 golf holes, such was the quality of the land. While making headway on a routing, the two realised some land required to tie it together existed just beyond a boundary fence (where the current 11th green and 16th tees were built, allowing holes 12 to 15 to exist). Coore and Crenshaw approached Youngscap about using this land, and he could be forgiven for thinking a request to use it was ridiculous (8,100 acres wasn't enough?) but he trusted the pair and was able to secure a land swap with the neighbouring landowner.

Construction began in April 1993. Equity to fund the construction came from fifteen investors, and the Sand Hills Golf Company was created with Dick Youngscap as managing member and director. Construction was cheap and simple; with Coore and Crenshaw's minimalist philosophy, hardly any dirt needed to be moved. The general approach for construction and grow-in was to mow down the existing vegetation on the desired playing areas, till (turn over) the soil to a depth of six inches, undertake minor finishing work (mostly to the greens with a power rake/sand pro), and then apply seed, fertiliser and water. In many cases, bunkers weren't shaped so much as roughly sculpted out of the landscape and left while other works were being completed to see what intricate detailing Mother Nature could come up with. The course is blessed to sit atop the Ogallala Aquifer – one of the world's largest aquifers – and sand that is well suited for turfgrass, with qualities that closely match it to USGA specification greens mix. This aided immensely in the construction and grow-in phases, with the course officially opening in June 1995.

Today, the course remains faithful to what was in the ground the day it opened, but keeping it that way isn't easy in this harsh environment. The man at the helm, ensuring this course accurately represents Coore and Crenshaw's vision, is Kyle Hegland. 'Most of our decisions are based on playability. We want the shots that Ben and Bill want you to hit, the shots that you can hit', Hegland says.

It's obvious when playing the course that the ground game is an important part of golf at Sand Hills. Ensuring surfaces remain firm and bouncy is one of the toughest jobs in a severe climate, where winter temperatures can drop below -20°C, and summer temperatures regularly top 30°C. Much of the responsibility for the playability of the course during the golfing season lies in work that's carried out during the harsh off-season. 'After working on bunkers we'll then go to top-dressing, which started as a winter health issue for the plant to protect them, but also firms up surfaces for the golf season. We're also one of the few places in the continental United States that gets turf desiccation, just because it gets so cold and so windy with massive temperature fluctuations. If it's dry and freezing, that means lots of winter watering, which isn't fun.' The fruits of Kyle and his team's labour are on full display during the golf season from late May through late September. The harsh winter winds are replaced by refreshing summer breezes, and with firm fescue fairways and surrounds, the course plays as true to a links course anywhere outside of the British Isles. My arrival at the club was via Denver, Colorado, the nearest city serviced by the main domestic airlines and some international carriers, despite being a five-hour drive. There are smaller regional airports nearer, but either way, Sand Hills is a long way from everywhere. Thankfully, it's a nice drive, with a good portion of the first half through an area known as the Colorado Chop Hills, home to Ballyneal Golf Club. Simply put, it's inspiring golf land. The drive gets more agricultural as you cross the border to Nebraska, but once you hit North Platte, the true Nebraska Sand Hills await. As you turn off Interstate 80 and down quieter roads, the only life above grass level are the occasional cattle dotted on the landscape. Their eyes follow my car as though I'm the only one to have passed in the last hour. Land quickly gets choppier and more interesting, with the driver's side more dramatic. I'm in a conflict of trying to arrive at Sand Hills as fast as I can or driving a little slower, peering out my window and allowing my mind to digest the landscape, finding a few green sites among the humps and hollows. I pass the occasional sandy blowout and ponder if these were the same ones Bill Coore saw on his drive to the site, ones that inspired those on the golf course?

My phone has no signal, but luckily the GPS location still works, and I'm navigated to a simple open gate with sculpted wire on one of its posts. The shapes look familiar. *SH*. I park my car and wander down to the clubhouse. I'm given a cart and told the rough directions to the course. It's a mile drive, and the range is on the way. Perfect. I hit a few balls to loosen my body after being cramped in my rental car for the last few hours. The first thing I notice is that the ball seems to hang in the air forever. Maybe it's the altitude (a little over 1,000 metres), or maybe it's the vast expanse of open prairieland forming a backdrop that creates the illusion of seemingly infinite hang time.

I'm met at the practice green by the assistant superintendent, Jarod. He's twenty-seven, but has thirteen years' experience at the club, first as a caddie during high school, then on the grounds crew. The golf club is the largest employer of the town, with many of the staff having been there since day one, including Jarod's mother. I knock a few putts to gauge the speed of the greens, and we head to the 1st tee.

The opening hole is a sweeping par-5. The sheer scale of the landscape makes it difficult to judge how far away the hazards are, and leaves a nagging uncertainty at the back of your mind on every shot. Thankfully, Jarod shows the way and we both safely land on the short grass. With a southerly wind, I'm able to reach the green in two, but miss short right in the greenside bunker, leaving one of the most challenging recovery shots on the golf course. I leave it in there and end up making a soft bogey.

The second hole plays up and over a broad hill to a brilliant plateaued green. The pin is high right on a tiny shelf, and I play what I think is a perfect pitch shot. I turn away to find my divot, only to look back and watch my ball slowly making its way down to the middle of the green, leaving a challenging putt. Walking up to the perched green, the stunning backdrop reveals itself – sand dunes as far as the eye can see.

On the par-3 3rd, Jarod shows me what thirteen years of experience looks like in a single golf shot. After missing the ball short right to a front right pin, he knocks the ball long left of the pin, only for the slopes to magically bring the ball back to within gimmie range.

Walking off the 4th green – the only truly 'man-made' green on the property – we head to the back tee for the 5th, which plays directly back over the 4th green, to a fairway that clearly favours shots played from the right-hand side. I veer safely left and am faced with a semi-blind approach to one of the smallest greens on the course.

Back-to-back short par-4s at the 7th and 8th may look easy on the card, but require precision play. The first of the two is a classic drivable hole, with more trouble the closer one tries to get to the green. The front left trap leaves an incredibly difficult bunker shot to a green that runs away, while going long right leaves a tricky pitch shot from fifteen feet below the surface of the green. Eight, on the other hand isn't drivable, but the boomerang-shaped green heavily dictates the desired angle into the green and therefore the desired line off the tee. I manage to drive one within thirty yards of the green, but too far right to a left pin and I need the talent of Phil Mickelson to get something to even hold the green. I execute well and am able to make a nice three.

As we make the turn, the sun begins to dip lower in the sky and clouds break away, revealing sunshine to highlight the native grasses across the stunning terrain. With two hours till sunset, we've timed our run perfectly. The 10th, 11th and 12th holes all sweep away from the clubhouse yet in vastly different ways. The 10th rolls its way down over beautiful tumbling topography to a green that accepts all manner of shots. The 11th plays downhill across a mammoth bunker to a perched green. I found myself taking too aggressive of a line and being bitten for it, leaving one of the toughest approach shots from a deep natural sandy ravine. The 12th plays over a hogsback fairway down to a hollow short of the green. After hitting what I thought was a perfect drive down the right side, I was left with a completely blind shot. A hole for the longer hitter to consider laying back to open up a better view of the target for their second shot.

Turning around to play the 13th, the most striking feature is its infinity green, which sits precariously on a hill with the pin framed by endless sky. Also visible from the tee is the approach to the 14th, which in my opinion may be the best of the bunch, on a course with more than a dozen holes that could battle for that prize. Reachable in two for many but to the smallest target on the course tucked away in the dunes, it requires a bold play to take it on, with the smartest leave just short left of the green over the large defending bunker.

Holes 15 through 18 meander their way back to the clubhouse, with 15 likely the hardest hole on the course, both for its length and the challenge of its green. Sixteen then plays off an elevated tee, offering views over most of the back nine and, importantly, the adventurous hole ahead. The final two holes are two of the best anywhere, with the postage stamp-like 17th requiring a lofted and precise short iron to the heavily guarded green. Reaching the green (hopefully in one shot), you'll be rewarded with a stunning view of the closing hole, a twisting climb to the green, with an iconic windmill reminding golfers of this courses' past. The final green is much like the first: a false-fronted green nestled among some dunes, offering forgiveness for approach shots played a little long. By the time we finish, moonlight is providing more illumination than the sun, which has settled below the horizon.

Following our round, Jarod and I retreat to Ben's Porch (named after Mr Crenshaw) and watch clouds roll in, covering the moonlight and replacing it with interspersed bursts of lightning in the distance. It's the perfect spot to reflect on one of the best days in golf.

Looking at Sand Hills retrospectively, it's easy to conclude that it was a turning point for golf course development in America and around the world. In an age when one residential development after another was being built, Sand Hills proved good golf could thrive not as an amenity, but as the star of the show. If the process of routing a golf course can be likened to solving a jigsaw puzzle, Sand Hills was a Rembrandt waiting to emerge. The only problem was, there were too many pieces and it was Bill Coore and Ben Crenshaw's job to find the right ones. Rather than jamming in ones that looked like a close fit, where it would be obvious something wasn't quite right, Coore and Crenshaw had the time and experience to solve the puzzle elegantly. With its success, Sand Hills became a proving ground of sorts for Mike Keiser who, as a founding member of the club, went on to open Bandon Dunes Golf Resort on the coast of Oregon, Cabot Links in Nova Scotia, and has played a part in the development of Barnbougle and Sand Valley (the latter with his sons). Although Sand Hills is a private golf club, Keiser took the Youngscap's remote golf model and applied it to the public arena. Thus, the broader golfing community is indebted to Sand Hills' existence, for had it not, it's unlikely any of the mentioned courses would exist either.

The course also represents a turning point for golf architecture. Sand Hills was a throwback to the classical principles of the golden age architects, which had long been forgotten or ignored. With the attention brought to it, there started a paradigm shift away from the bland, cookie-cutter golf design that had plagued the United States and other parts of the globe. With it started a neoclassical era of golf design that we're fortunate to be living through today.

INSIDER'S GUIDE TO PINEHURST NORTH CAROLINA, USA

WORDS BY SHAUN TOLSON
PHOTOGRAPHY BY MATT CARDIS
AND CHRISTIAN HAFER

Over the course of 125 years, Pinehurst Resort has steadily grown into the cradle of American golf – always expanding, always adapting, always offering an authentic golfing experience for players of all ability levels.

An American Evolution

In the early evening hours of the second Sunday of summer, tranquillity has overtaken the covered porch of the Carolina Hotel in Pinehurst Resort. In one corner, a classical guitarist quietly tunes his instrument in preparation for a performance, while guests sip libations and recline in white-painted rocking chairs that look out over the hotel's circular lawn. Amid this idyllic scene, collegiate golfers shouldering lightweight bags branded with their schools' logos intermittently return to the hotel following practice rounds for the North & South Men's Amateur, a prestigious championship first contested in 1901, which will begin in two days' time.

A hotel transport van returns from the airport, pulling up under the hotel's portico. The van's sliding door opens and eight middle-aged men enthusiastically spill out. Suitcases are removed from the cargo hold, bags are claimed and transferred to luggage carts, and those carts are left in the care of the hotel's bellmen. During this shuffling of belongings, golf bags are removed from their travel cases, shoes are changed and the eight travellers – many of whom have not yet stepped inside the hotel – climb aboard a smaller shuttle, clubs in tow and golf gloves already on, chirping about the stakes of their impending matches.

'This is the new Pinehurst, a relaxed and comfortable golf destination, which has made a discreet but undeniable transformation in recent years.'

As the sun dips low, bathing the Sand Hills of North Carolina in copper and golden hues of light, the posse of golfers hurries off for a twilight round at The Cradle, the resort's fledgling short course. There they'll be interspersed with families and other avid golfers like themselves – playing casual or perhaps competitive rounds – all while an eclectic mix of music plays from a collection of speakers artfully camouflaged and strategically placed across the course's ten acres.This is the new Pinehurst, a relaxed and comfortable golf destination, which has made a discreet but undeniable transformation in recent years. Through the creation of the aforementioned Cradle, this once-traditional golf mecca has loosened up and, in doing so, has broadened its appeal to a younger crowd. But the Pinehurst of old – the bastion of American golf history – still exists, as a tour of the Carolina Hotel shows. Though it also delivers proof that the resort's perspective and approach to its history has changed too.

History on Display

A step inside the Carolina Hotel is not only an immersion into the history of American golf; it's an immersion into the history of American society. Hanging from the walls of the grand hotel's main hallway – as well as in the lobby, the hallways of the upper floors and on the landings in each of the hotel's stairwells – are more than 200 photos, prints and paintings, all of which play a role in recounting the resort's century-long story. Just before guests reach the main hallway, a welcome message hangs adjacent to the check-in desk, introducing hotel guests to the artwork and the snapshots in time that surround them. It reads:

For as long as Pinehurst has been a beloved home of golf in America, the Carolina Hotel has been our living room.

Since 1895, Pinehurst has been a destination for people escaping the hectic pace of the everyday, a peaceful respite proud to be known as the cradle of golf in America.

Traditions define our past and guide our future, where for more than a century visionaries, dignitaries and people like you have defined Pinehurst's history.

Historical displays among these walls reflect some of our favourite stories and, we hope, some of yours, too.

The message was penned by golf historian David Normoyle, who was hired almost four years ago to oversee the redesign of the hotel's public spaces. More specifically, Normoyle was brought in to help the hotel better tell its story as the central gathering place – the living room – of Pinehurst Resort. 'From a design standpoint, it is my job to understand what a club or a resort is and to help them express their story and their environment in a way that makes people not know that I was ever there,' he says. 'My job is not to provide good answers, but to ask questions that yield good answers.'

When Normoyle first arrived at the hotel, he quickly perceived how its ambiance was failing. It looked dated. 'You can be classic or you can be contemporary, which is equally appealing to people in different ways,' he explains. 'But you can't be dated. You can't be stuck in the middle. That's where things start to feel tired.' In Normoyle's assessment, the hotel's interior reflected two distinct time periods: the turn of the 20th century (when the hotel was built) and the present moment.

Normoyle's intention was to blur that sense of time. He wanted to capture the significance of the hotel and its place within the resort's grand narrative. He wanted guests 'to feel the pulse of history' as they walked down the hotel's hallways. And he wanted to do it in a manner that felt timeless. 'From the moment you walk in the lobby and as you're walking down the halls – the central nervous system of the place – you want to know without a shadow of a doubt that you're at Pinehurst,' he says, 'but you want it to be slightly unclear what year it is.'

To accomplish that, Normoyle dove into Pinehurst's vast archives. He sifted through thousands of photographs and, as he acknowledges, only the most superlative images made the cut. 'Every picture on every wall is there for an exact and specific reason,' he declares, adding that the intention was to create an emotional effect, one that resonated with people, but one that also provided them with information if they were inquisitive.

'I wanted to make the hallway experience at the Carolina be like a field guide to what Pinehurst is all about,' Normoyle acknowledges. 'But if all you want to do is walk around and think, "This is a pleasant place and those are cool photos and I'm glad I'm here," that's good enough.'

A casual walk down the Carolina's main hallway brings chapters of the resort's story into focus. Sepia-toned photos of the hotel itself, including images of its lobby, game room, parlours and verandah, offer guests a glimpse of bygone eras of hospitality. Snapshots of dignitaries and US presidents at the hotel and on the resort's golf courses convey the allure that has attracted affluent and discerning travellers to Pinehurst for more than a hundred years. And a century-old image of three resort guests – a lady with a tennis racquet, a polo player with a mallet and a golfer with a hickory-shafted driver – reflects the various recreational pursuits that have long served as a foundation of the resort's overall experience.

As the aforementioned photograph suggests, images and advertisements prominently spotlight female guests enjoying the hotel and many of the resort's amenities, golf included. Those are some of Normoyle's favourites, because they contend that women have been a central fixture of life at Pinehurst since the resort's founding. They also affirm that Pinehurst has always been a welcoming place for the game of golf and all groups of people who love to play it.

Those who wish to discover additional stories of the resort, its courses, hotels and life inside the village of Pinehurst can visit the same archives that Normoyle utilised. A ten-minute walk through the village brings hotel guests to the Given Memorial Library and Tufts Archives, where hundreds of thousands of images are on file, not to mention several hundred thousand documents and newspaper clippings. 'It's pretty much a Pinehurst history museum,' executive director Audrey Moriarty says.

According to Moriarty, guests who spend thirty minutes walking through the archives will learn enough of the resort's early beginnings, including its creation story, to discover that the cradle of American golf was conceived without plans to ever build a golf course. The resort and village's founder, James Walker Tufts, sold a prosperous soda fountain company in Boston and purchased 5,800 acres of forested pineland in the Sandhills of North Carolina with the intention of building a New England-style health retreat. Although Tufts envisioned numerous recreational activities to be offered, it was only at the request of guests – three years after Pinehurst's first hotel, The Holly Inn, opened – that a rudimentary nine-hole golf course was constructed.

With one of Tufts' soda fountains on display, along with an original map of the village, visitors to the archives can better appreciate that genesis. Yet, as one might expect, the vast majority of artefacts, memorabilia and documentation within the Tufts Archives focuses on golf. 'You can't really talk too much about Pinehurst without talking about golf,' Moriarty acknowledges.

In that respect, the Tufts Archives is as much a memorial to Donald Ross as it is a tribute to the village of Pinehurst and the resort that was built alongside it. The archives feature the largest collection of Ross's original drawings and course blueprints, which contemporary course architects (Gil Hanse, Bill Coore, Ben Crenshaw and others) have studied ahead of restoration projects. Notebooks containing reproductions of the field sketches that Ross made throughout his career are also available to guests.

Yet the Tufts Archives' most eye-catching tribute to the late course designer is a collection of flags taken from Ross-designed courses around the country. These flags, in bold primary colours, are displayed in three rows along the upper portion of the archives' walls and form a complete ring around the room. As impressive a sight as that is, there are hundreds more of them that are filed away in drawers. The flags, as Moriarty has observed, create personal connections for many of the golf enthusiasts who visit the archives. 'It allows them to relive their own golf history,' she says.

Much of the resort's history connected to Pinehurst's revered No. 2 course is proudly displayed in prominent places throughout the resort's main clubhouse. In glass display windows running the length of the main hallway, for example, autographed golf bags, advertising posters and pin flags chronicle the Ryder Cup matches of 1951, the US Senior Open of 1994 and the 2008 US Amateur Championship, among the many other notable championships and events that have been contested there. The 1999 US Open – the first US Open played at Pinehurst – is celebrated and memorialised on the grandest scale with a dedicated alcove; however, one curious piece of memorabilia from that championship is displayed somewhere else.

'It was a misty June day,' Pinehurst Resort's president Tom Pashley recalls of the Sunday when that championship's final round was played. 'Misty enough to need a rain jacket but warm enough to not want to wear rain gear.' Payne Stewart, the championship's eventual winner, stopped by the Paget Learning Center on his way to warm up on the range and asked to borrow a pair of scissors. With those scissors in hand, Stewart promptly cut the sleeves off of his rain jacket just above the elbow. 'For him to take scissors to GoreTex during the final round of the US Open is crazy,' Pashley says.

Stewart tossed the cut-off sleeves in the trash, but someone on the Paget Center staff retrieved them. Today, those sleeves are displayed on the back wall of The Deuce pub, just above the buffet station. Pashley is the first to acknowledge that the sleeves deserve better placement, and he asserts that they'll be relocated eventually. 'But for now,' he says, 'you have to look behind the buffet to see one of the coolest items that we have.'

Golfing by the Numbers

From a golf standpoint, the No. 2 course has shone brightly as Pinehurst's crown jewel since the mid-1930s. Spread out over 196 acres, the course has captivated golf enthusiasts of all ability levels for the better part of a century. During that time, it has also challenged (and sufficiently frustrated) the world's best players, beginning in 1936, when Pinehurst hosted the PGA Championship, the first of six major championships that have been contested there to date.

Widely considered to be Donald Ross's pièce de résistance, the No. 2 course underwent a comprehensive restoration conducted by Bill Coore and Ben Crenshaw in 2010 – one that replaced lush Bermuda rough with native sandscape, shrinking the amount of grassed turf on the course by twenty-six acres but increasing the size of the course's fairways by thirteen acres. As Coore acknowledges, the restored layout now looks and plays in a manner that would please the course's original creator were he alive to see it, although one modern aspect likely would catch Ross's eye.

In the 1940s, the greens on the No. 2 course featured subtle yet intricate internal contours. Over the subsequent decades, the greens have slowly increased in height, which Coore attributes to the repetitive maintenance practice of top-dressing the putting surfaces with sand. 'If you add just a quarter of an inch of sand on a putting surface countless times over many, many decades,' he says, 'the greens build up, and they build up significantly.'

As the greens have increased in height, many of those subtle contours have disappeared. Yet, in the process, the crowned greens, with their steeply sloped edges, have become one of the No. 2 course's defining features. 'Pinehurst is so revered for what it is now in terms of those crowned greens,' says Coore. 'People talk about how precise you have to be around the greens with your chipping and putting. The greens are at the forefront of numerous reasons why it's such a good competition golf course.'

With that in mind, the course architects charged with the restoration of the famous No. 2 course recognised that its modern greens are as important as many other original design features lost over time. It was those reclaimable features that became their focus.

Although initially built in 1907, the No. 2 course is one that evolved steadily through the decades; and for the first forty years of the course's existence, it was Donald Ross himself who steered those transformations. In Coore's estimation, the version of the No. 2 course that 'captured the golf world's imagination' is the one that existed for three decades, from 1935 until the late 1960s. 'That's the version of No. 2 that we hoped to restore.'

To do that, Coore and Crenshaw heavily relied on two guiding beacons. They first traced the main irrigation line down the centre of every fairway, which helped them to determine the original width of those fairways (and their original shape). They also referenced aerial photographs taken by the US Air Force in 1943 as a part of World War II reconnaissance missions flown over nearby Fort Bragg. 'Ben and I made the assumption that by 1943, Ross had the No. 2 course the way he wanted it,' Coore explains.

The reintroduction of those sandscapes completely altered the course's aesthetic, not to mention the playing experiences that it provides, and they are vital to the course's authenticity. 'He referred to it as the most perfect rough,' Coore says, referencing Donald Ross's documented opinion of the native playing areas that originally extended beyond the perimeter of the fairway. 'It was the unpredictability of it. You could have a really good lie or a really not good lie. You just didn't know as you watched your ball roll into that stuff. I think he appreciated that. I know Ben and I appreciated that and the naturalness of it.

'Pinehurst is a throwback to what golf was when it was a game played in nature and not a botanical garden,' Coore continues. 'If you play a course like No. 2, most often every round something memorable is going to occur. That memorable moment may be really happy and positive, and it may be the exact opposite. There's that element of unpredictability. It's the element of the unknown. That's the thrill. It's what's captured people's imaginations for hundreds of years about playing golf.'

It's easy to simply say that the unpredictability of the No. 2 course is part of its charm, but that does little to prepare those who have yet to experience the course. So, what is it like to play a round on the No. 2 course?

‘Pinehurst is a throwback to what golf was when it was a game played in nature and not a botanical garden.’

‘The fairways are forty or fifty yards wide. There’s no out-of-bounds. There’s no water. You think you could scrape it around without making any double bogeys?’ asks Bob Farren, Pinehurst’s vice-president of golf course maintenance. According to Farren, a lot of first-time players on the No. 2 course will confidently say yes. ‘You’d win a lot of money making bets on that,’ he laughs, ‘because you will make a double bogey.

‘Even during your round, you play six holes and you think, “Dang, I had a chance to make birdie there and par there. Here I am five-over and I feel like I should be even par,”’ Farren continues. ‘More than any course here that people play, when they come in and start counting their regrets they probably have the most of them on No 2.’

When first asked what it’s like to play a round on the No. 2 course, caddie Thomas Trinchitella, one of the resort’s longest-tenured loopers, answers with more ambiguity than clarity. ‘It’s indescribable,’ he says. ‘You couldn’t go play No. 2 and then describe [to someone who hasn’t played the course] the good and the bad that happened to you. They wouldn’t understand it.

‘You hit the best shot of your life,’ Trinchitella says, expounding on his initial statement, ‘and you’re twenty feet off the green even though it landed five feet short of the flagstick. That sort of thing happens on every shot.’

Trinchitella also points out that first-time players of the No. 2 course often quickly revert to despair when they hit a shot that lands in or rolls into the native sandscapes. ‘It [often] looks a lot worse from a distance than what it actually is,’ he says. ‘There’s more space and more spaces to stand [than you think], and there are more times when you’ll have a good lie versus a bad lie.’

Players can request specific caddies ahead of their rounds on any of Pinehurst’s courses, and those who are lucky enough to walk a course with Trinchitella can spend the time chatting with him about his experiences caddying for dignitaries, such as US President George H W Bush, and also some of the best players in the world – a list that includes Tiger Woods, Rory McIlroy and Annika Sörenstam.

HOLE 2
PAR 4
YDS 411
PINEHURST
No. 2

Players who have Trinchitella on their bag for a round on the No. 2 course can also expect the long-time caddie to offer suggestions, both on shots to be hit and possible celebratory acts to perform. Should one of Trinchitella's players have a putt for par on the 18th hole, for example, the caddie will encourage them, if they make it, to re-enact Payne Stewart's famous fist pump from the 1999 US Open.

On the topic of that 18th hole, players should also know that their shots coming in will not go unnoticed, especially later in the day. The patio outside The Deuce teems with people, many enjoying a meal or beverages, and the entertainment that's offered those patrons most often takes the form of the groups of golfers playing the final hole. 'As people come up the 18th fairway, everyone is picking their player as the one who wins this hole,' he says. 'They get pulled into watching what happens on 18. It's the perfect place for people watching.'

According to Pashley, the perfect place to enjoy a post-round cocktail of your own is half a mile away from The Deuce's patio in a halfway house named The Nest, which was modelled after Pinehurst's original clubhouse, circa 1898. It sits on a small ridge at a junction where the No. 2 and No. 4 courses briefly meet. There, visitors can enjoy an exclusive cocktail named after the red-cockaded woodpecker, which inhabits the area. The Nest also offers unparalleled views.

> 'When played using modern equipment, the historic layout becomes an exercise in restraint and course management.'

Although much of the attention is rightfully paid to Pinehurst's No. 2 course, the other eight eighteen-hole layouts each offer their own appeals. The aforementioned No. 4 course, for example, benefited from a comprehensive redesign by Gil Hanse in 2018 and now offers a more audacious playing experience than the neighbouring No. 2, albeit one that shares an aesthetic punctuated by those same native sandscapes. 'It's a lot of the same texture, the same fabric and DNA as No. 2,' says Farren. 'No. 2 is more subtle. No. 4 is more of a bold, large-scale landscape.'

Players who venture down the fairways of the No. 1 course will encounter a replica springhouse, built in 2011, that pays homage to The Tin Whistles, an organisation of amateur golfers founded in 1904, which included Donald Ross. And across the ninety holes that span courses No. 5 through No. 9, players will see how some of golf's most successful course architects (Rees Jones, Tom Fazio, Jack Nicklaus and others) have left their own marks on the Sandhills of North Carolina.

Simply put, players who tee up on one of the resort's many courses will discover the diverse golfing experience that Pinehurst provides. 'No. 2 brings you here,' Trinchitella says, 'and the other courses bring you back.'

Hickory-shafted Time Machines

The one course in Pinehurst Resort's vast lineup that is most often overlooked by guests is the No. 3 course. Described (and touted) by the resort as 'short but mighty', the No. 3 course measures slightly more than 5,000 yards – 5,155 yards, to be exact – and was designed by Donald Ross in 1910, though the course benefited from a restoration and subtle redesign in 2017.

When played using modern equipment, the historic layout becomes an exercise in restraint and course management. Drivers – even 3-woods – are unlikely to be pulled from most players' bags with any regularity. Instead, long irons and hybrids represent the clubs of choice for players off the tee on many of the course's ten par-4s and its two par-5s.

When played using hickory clubs, however, the No. 3 course shines for its ability to transport players to a bygone era of American golf; and through the resort's hickory club rental program, guests can easily take that step back in time. Leaving their bulky stand or cart bags at the caddie office, players slip a lightweight Jones carry bag over their shoulders. Inside that bag, eight modern hickory-shafted clubs – all of them Tad Moore Hickory Classics – will present those adventurous golfers with a slew of new challenges (and new experiences). The set's 12-degree Pall Mall Hickory Driver – a club patterned after a popular driver made by Scotsman William Gibson in the early 20th century – features a sweet spot no larger than an American quarter, while the 48-degree mashie niblick lacks the type of bounce that contemporary wedges provide.

No matter the club in a player's hands, Pinehurst's head golf pro, Matt Barksdale, offers one critical piece of advice. 'Swing easy,' he says. 'The shafts get so much bend and create so much spin on the ball ... the moment you try to get after it, the ball gets very spinny. It will hook or slice dramatically.'

Aside from challenging golfers and testing their abilities to think creatively, Pinehurst's hickory rental program excels for its ability to reshape those golfers' perspective about the game and its history. 'It's a fun experience for individuals who have never done it and also for people who might play hickories once or twice a year,' Barksdale says of renting a set and playing the No.1 course, the No. 3 course, or The Cradle. 'They go out there with no expectations whatsoever and simply enjoy the game. It will give them a fresh perspective of Bobby Jones and Walter Hagen and Old Tom Morris. It gives everybody a true appreciation for the early years of golf and how talented those individuals really were.'

Short and Sweet

Just beyond the walking path on the southern side of the resort's main clubhouse extends a sprawling swath of closely mown turf gradually trundling downhill and sporting a bevy of humps and miniature hillocks. This is Pinehurst's ten-acre Thistle Dhu putting course, a feature that draws comparisons to the famed Himalayas putting course located a stone's throw from the 2nd tee of The Old Course in St Andrews, and home to the St Andrews Ladies' Putting Club. The course name pays homage to a putting course built at the home of James Barber, owner of a New York steamship company, who moved to Pinehurst in 1919. As legend has it, upon seeing his completed home and putting course, Barber exclaimed, 'This'll do.' That statement was later spelled Thistle Dhu and the name, as they say, stuck.

The course inspires – one could say it even fosters – a sense of revelry. Laughter forms the foundation of Thistle Dhu's soundtrack, and it's not uncommon for players to make their way around the course barefoot. Even the course's tee markers, which double as a duo of cup holders, promote gaiety. 'If they were crossed hickory clubs, that would be telling you one thing,' Pashley acknowledges, 'but the drink holders tell you that we're expecting you to have fun and encouraging you to have fun.'

Only 150 yards from Pinehurst's famous Putter Boy statue, which rests at the centre of the Thistle Dhu course, sits the 1st tee of The Cradle. Not unlike the putting course, laughter and jovial banter fill the air of this nine-hole short course, the concealed speakers placed throughout the grounds providing a true soundtrack for play, one made up of an eclectic mix of classic rock and contemporary pop hits.

The two courses are the handiwork of Gil Hanse and Jim Wagner, who were given the opportunity to put shovels in the earth ahead of their redesign of the No. 4 course in 2018. It would be an understatement to simply declare the courses a success; in fact, many suggest that they are the catalysts of Pinehurst's positive transformation. 'Tons of credit goes to Gil and Jim,' Pashley says, 'for creating something that's fun, that's stimulating to a scratch player and welcoming to a beginner, and something that can be played with only a putter if that's what you want to do.'

The resort had considered building a short course for several years prior to Hanse and Wagner breaking ground on The Cradle. Initially, considerations were made to create one at the site of The Pit Golf Links, a golf course that the resort acquired in 2011. The location would provide plenty of land to make it happen, but it was deemed to be too far from the nucleus of the resort.

Building it where they did, although prominently on display and easily accessible, presented its own challenges and anxieties. Most notably, it meant that the first holes on both the No. 3 course and the No. 5 course had to be moved. In the process, par for the No. 3 course would drop two strokes, from seventy to sixty-eight. These were significant changes that Pashley worried would anger the golf purists who visited the resort and revered its history.

Pashley was also concerned that the courses, specifically the Thistle Dhu hummocks and moguls, would mar the stately appearance of the clubhouse. In reality, they did nothing of the sort. Instead, the two courses produced a destination where golfing parents can bring their children without the worry that their kids won't conform to the decorum that defines so many golf clubs. 'To have a course where they can come and roll down the hill if they want ... they can burst out in laughter and be a part of everyone else who is doing it, it makes so much sense now and it speaks to the transformation that has happened at Pinehurst in small ways,' Pashley says. 'It's liberating now to bring them out here and let them loose.'

That such a place exists only 900 feet away from the starter's hut for the No. 4 course and 700 feet away from the 1st tee of the No. 2 course is an even greater accomplishment. As Pashley acknowledges, 'The Cradle is 789 yards that has done more to redefine what Pinehurst stands for than anything else that we've done.'

'The course inspires – one could say it even fosters – a sense of revelry. Laughter forms the foundation of Thistle Dhu's soundtrack, and it's not uncommon for players to make their way around the course barefoot.'

What the Future Holds

A glance back in time offers some indication of what's to come for Pinehurst as the resort continues its evolution. Visitors' immediate acceptance of The Cradle and Thistle Dhu courses paved the way for new developments, like The Nest, to take form. 'The acceptance of the new energy and the fun factor that The Cradle and Thistle Dhu created and seeing how much people were enjoying it emboldened us to try some new things,' Pashley says. 'The fact that people were embracing it and celebrating it and saying that Pinehurst was transitioning from being a little stodgy to being kind of cool and fun, it made us want to continue to push ourselves.'

More than one million visitors travel to Pinehurst on an annual basis, yet that's a number that could conceivably rise. The USGA has announced that it will establish a Golf House Pinehurst, which would include an equipment-testing facility, a museum and a visitor's centre. Additionally, Pinehurst was named the first anchor site for the US Open, which will bring the major championship to the resort's famed No. 2 course every five or six years.

'Even before, you could sit on the front porch of the Carolina Hotel and the world of golf would pass through those doors,' says Pashley. 'Now there's going to be a steady introduction of Pinehurst to the next generation of golfers every five or six years.'

As one of the United States' four national landmarks in golf – and the only one accessible to the public – Pinehurst Resort will always attract a segment of golf travellers simply due to its rich history. Yet the resort's commitment to evolve, to reinvent itself to stay relevant to younger generations, is what will keep the resort at the forefront of avid golfers' minds, no matter their age. Looking back on the resort's history, it becomes clear that is something the resort has done steadily for the better part of 120 years.

'It's the story of generations upon generations of leaders trying ideas on for size and being willing to keep the ones that stick and being willing to reject the ones that don't,' Normoyle says of the resort's steady growth. 'There's no place in America like it.'

TWO BRIDGES TOO FAR

WORDS BY HAL PHILLIPS WITH TOM DOAK
PHOTOGRAPHY BY TOM DOAK
AND WILLIAM WATT

Even the world's greatest architects have their white whales. For Tom Doak, it's a course he never built below Cape Kidnappers – a rough-hewn, sheep-grazed treasure that would complement his acclaimed clifftop masterpiece. Two river canyons and their million-dollar bridges stand between dream and reality.

Would-be developers don't often possess surfeits of stellar terrain. Even a veritable visionary with unlimited funds and lofty aspirations might serve up only twenty-five to fifty acres of superior, sandy routing fodder; the rest is something with which a course architect makes do. However, when it comes to matters such as these, Tom Doak is the wrong person to ask. Part of his genius has been the ability – or serial good fortune – to connect with developers not just with great land but thousands and thousands of acres of great land.

Convincing clients what to build on any piece of ground is central to the modern course design exercise, and not even Doak gets his way every time. The man is human, and over his long and decorated career, these courses not taken are what pass for professional regrets. In his 2020 book, *Getting to 18*, Doak cites one in particular, 'the project I most regret not having gotten the chance to design.

'The very first time I went to Cape Kidnappers was the end of 2001, and I was late,' the architect said, referring to his world-beating design on New Zealand's North Island, developed by American billionaire Julian Robertson. 'They picked me up in a helicopter and landed me on the point down below, where you can see the Shark's Tooth. At that time, Julian wanted to build his lodge down there and, in my opinion – then and now – that would have been a superb place to build a golf course. It was flat enough, to go with plenty of acreage. From the moment the helicopter touched down, I was like, "Why wouldn't we build it down here in this valley?"

'It didn't take long for Julian to make himself clear: the clifftops were his first choice and it's hard to argue. His vision for golf on those cliffs was inspired. It's a setting like no other. But I thought then – and I still think – a very good golf course could have gone down there in the valley.'

Cape Kidnappers earned its modern name after locals attempted to abduct a member of Captain Cook's crew aboard the HMS *Endeavour* after making landfall there on 15 October 1769. As is often the case, the Māori appellation for this sandstone headland, *Te Kauwae-a-Māui*, is far more evocative. And sacred. According to aboriginal teaching, the peninsula represents a fishhook used to pull the entire North Island out of the sea. The presence of Shark's Tooth Rock – a lonely piece of sandstone isolated and sharpened by aeons of wave-enabled erosion – capably underlines this visceral mythic imagery.

Of course, Robertson did ultimately develop Cape Kidnappers on the higher ground, above the famous chalk-white cliffs that rise some 500 feet above the waters of Hawke's Bay. He created the adjoining lodge, The Farm at Cape Kidnappers, on ground that was higher still. Doak's course, laid out ingeniously atop those clifftops, debuted in 2004. The ensuing decades have witnessed the debut of dozens more top-calibre designs (and high-class renovation work) from the likes of Hanse Golf Design, Coore & Crenshaw, Doak himself and myriad others. Cape Kidnappers is still ranked among the finest fifty tracks on the planet.

Robertson passed away in August 2022; his family continues to own and operate the property, which occupies some 6,000 acres on this stunning landform, across Hawke's Bay from New Zealand's finest wine region. Where Doak had envisioned that original course, thousands of sheep and steer roam and graze the landscape. The forbidding terrain directly above the Shark's Tooth remains home to the largest gannet colony in the southern hemisphere.

In 2020, when the architect returned to regrass the putting surfaces, he was refamiliarised with this extraordinary setting and reminded of the road not taken, the course he didn't end up building – a layout he refers to as The Farm.

'We would take picnic lunches down there when Cape Kidnappers was being built,' he recalls. 'I think it was our second trip when we gave Julian and his wife Josie a tour of the place. We had spent a few days on site just sticking flags in the ground – to show what the golf course could be. I think I undersold it back then. Julian's focus was always on building a top-100 golf course, whereas, at The Farm, Bruce [Hepner] and I were thinking more about a course with sheep and cows all over it. Which is what they use the land for now, of course. That's what so many "country courses" do, all over New Zealand.

'I don't honestly remember when Bruce and I went back and tried to actually *route* something down there,' Doak continues, referring to his former associate. 'It may have been 2008, when business was a lot slower. We had played around with maps from the start, but that was definitely our impetus – to get Julian more interested in a second course down below.'

When Doak arrived in New Zealand back in 2001, the architect had just embarked on a run of work for clients with ungodly amounts of terrific, sandy terrain – what some might call his Intercontinental Embarrassment of Riches Tour. At that time, he was fresh off his design of Pacific Dunes, located at Bandon Dunes in coastal Oregon, where Mike Keiser started out with some 2,000 acres of coastal terrain. Today, the resort is seven courses to the good and Keiser still hasn't worked through it all. In 2013, Doak christened the first of four courses at the 16,000-acre Streamsong Resort in central Florida. Today, he's working with still more Keisers at the 9,000-acre Sand Valley Resort in Wisconsin, where Doak's Lido homage has taken up residence beside his heathland design, Sedge Valley.

The architect also returned to New Zealand in 2013 to design and build Tara Iti Golf Club. It was this project that, in a roundabout way, first rekindled Doak's interest in The Farm course at Cape Kidnappers. The private seaside Tara Iti debuted in 2015, but its principals had also acquired yet another massive, adjacent parcel that stretched some ten kilometres down the beach. At Te Arai Links, the South Course, designed by Coore & Crenshaw, opened in early 2023 and the North Course, designed by Doak, opened in May 2024.

At the turn of the century, Doak's idea of building a second course at Cape Kidnappers was frankly a bit fanciful, the stuff of picnic whimsy. Today, pushing the limits of middle age, he is more focused on the projects that matter to him.

'I've not discussed it with anyone there at Cape, not formally. But maybe the Robertsons would think differently about it today – *because* of what's been happening up at Te Arai. I don't lie awake at night thinking about it, but I can tell you we'd jump at the chance to design and build a course down there. I don't know that there is the will to do it today, but maybe what's happening at Te Arai has upped the ante some.'

Golf in New Zealand dates back to the late 19th century, but it has come to be defined – internationally, in the 21st century – by a veritable gaggle of world-class dream tracks. Indeed, the Robertsons get credit for starting this opulent trend with the 1999 christening of Kauri Cliffs, which is located some 500 kilometres north of Cape Kidnappers and continues to occupy its own sub-tropical place in the world top-100.

Prior to this lux influx, Kiwi golf was better known for producing 1963 British Open champion Sir Bob Charles, and the nation's unique collection of so-called country or 'sheep' courses. Nothing could be further from Cape or Kauri Cliffs than these purposely casual, rough-hewn layouts, most of them modestly funded and originally built by locals driving their own DC3 Oliver tractors. Many lie well off the beaten track and double as grazing pasture, complete with fencing around the greens to protect them from the cloven hoofs of creatures bovine and ovine.

These country courses serve up a polar-opposite brand of golf to Cape Kidnappers or Tara Iti. And that's exactly what Doak and his colleagues have always had in mind for The Farm.

'First of all, that's the way *all* golf courses started out, in the beginning,' Doak points out. 'The only reason the Scots founded golf was, they had the land grazed – so you could play around and find the balls. Brora [in Scotland] is much like that still today, though someone else owns the grazing rights there, not the club. I hope they never take the animals away; that's always been part of the charm.'

Doak explained that when he and his crews were building Cape Kidnappers, all these displaced American design nerds became enamoured of a sheep course just down the coast. 'A really rough little thing. My guys loved it, though it may have since closed. [Wairunga GC did, in fact, cease operations circa 2018] … When my crew was building Tara Iti, my crew fell in love with another charming little course called Waverly, which was just named one of the top-100 courses in Asia–Pacific! I mean, how many votes they truly got as part of that ballot process, who can say? But I love the fact that all around Waverly, on that ranking, you have places like Haesley Nine Bridges [in South Korea] and all these other one-hundred-million-dollar developments!'

In thirty-plus years designing golf courses, Doak has proved far more than a course architect. Through his design capabilities and his writing, even the odd post on a website, he is seen as something of an evangelist for treeless/minimalist design styles, for the merits of 19th-century golf, for layouts that might otherwise operate in total obscurity. In 2018, for example, he praised Waverly GC in the pages of his *Confidential Guide to Golf Courses, Vol 5*. Located three miles from the Tasman Sea, clear across the North Island from Cape, WGC has since taken on something approaching cult status, compete with regional rankings and pilgrimages from far-flung Doak acolytes. Ironically, I have it on good authority that Waverly has gone ahead and planted a bunch of trees along some of its previously unadorned fairways. According to one member, this was undertaken so that when Tom Doak comes back, 'We will look like a proper golf course, with trees!'

'In thirty-plus years designing golf courses, Doak has proved far more than a course architect. Through his design capabilities and his writing, even the odd post on a website, he is seen as something of an evangelist for treeless/minimalist design styles, for the merits of 19th-century golf, for layouts that might otherwise operate in total obscurity.'

'When I went to Waverly,' Doak says, 'there was nobody there in the tiny clubhouse. We went in the locker room to see if there was *some*one to pay. Nope. But there were all these signs: *No Golf Shoes in Clubhouse. Why so precious?* we all wondered. Well, there's a balance. You can get the fairways playing pretty good with sheep all over them. But they produce a lot of shit, and folks don't want that in the clubhouse. It's a fine line.'

All faeces aside, modern folk might be surprised at just how practical and playable New Zealand's country golf model can be. For starters, putting surfaces are maintained more or less to modern standards, but for the fencing. Even with sheep on the job, fairways *are* mowed, if less frequently. Under these conditions, decent turf can be maintained – typically without any irrigation, especially in temperate climates like New Zealand's North Island. Golfers spoiled by 21st-century conditions may not realise it, but turfgrasses adapt quite well to natural weather variations and/or livestock-induced trauma. Indeed, those plants that cannot adapt will die off, allowing hardier varieties to take their place.

This is part of the lasting allure of The Farm, so far as Doak is concerned. Where else could one develop a 19th-century course on such superb terrain and place it beside something so magnificently modern and manicured as Cape Kidnappers? It's not that one track would prove better or more enjoyable than the other; rather, their wildly divergent experiences would complement, contrast and enhance one another.

Any discussion of the eighteen holes Doak and Hepner routed at The Farm back in 2008 must hinge on the land itself. The vast Cape Kidnappers property occupies the entire peninsula, yet much of the most suitable golfing terrain, existing and proposed, occupies a west-facing portion that overlooks Hawke's Bay. Aerial photos confirm Doak's first impressions upon landing in that helicopter: closer to sea level and north of his 2004 layout, three relatively level parcels are divided up by two river valleys that meet before flowing as one into the sea. Together, as Doaks routing attests, all three lobes would accommodate eighteen exceptional golf holes.

'I could see starting close to the existing course and working down into that valley,' Doak says. 'It's pretty steep, and we never did figure out a practical way to get down there [from the existing clubhouse]. But if you take the road out there, it goes along the edge of the clifftops. Where it does that, you've got a view of the first lobe, out to the point, with the Shark's Tooth in the distance. Our 1st hole would start there, a short par-5: You'd hit over the corner of the river and down to the flat. Probably a pretty hard opening hole but one of the great opening holes in golf. Very dramatic.

'The second hole is par-3 back over the ravine that flanks no. 1: 150 yards with a one-hundred-yard carry. Holes 3 through 8 are all on that side of the big river that winds through that piece of property. Nine plays diagonally across the same river to another lobe of this property, and that's the second bridge we'd require.

'I thought some of the coolest land was over on that lobe, 10 to 14. They'd be parallel holes, in a field basically, but the tee for 10 sits on a point with the river wrapping around it: an Alps hole on a pretty crazy scale. I remember a *really* good green site at 11, while 13 is a short dogleg around the base of a mountain, with just enough room for a fairway – and a green wrapping around the back of it. Crazy dramatic hole there.

'From there you had to take another bridge, then the 2nd hole bridge, to reach 15 tee. That fairway then plays out to the point where Julian wanted the lodge originally. We thought about just ending there, and we *could* do it differently. But we had 18 coming back inland from there.'

'Where else could one develop a 19th-century course on such superb terrain and place it beside something so magnificently modern and manicured as Cape Kidnappers? It's not that one track would prove better or more enjoyable than the other; rather, their wildly divergent experiences would complement, contrast and enhance one another.'

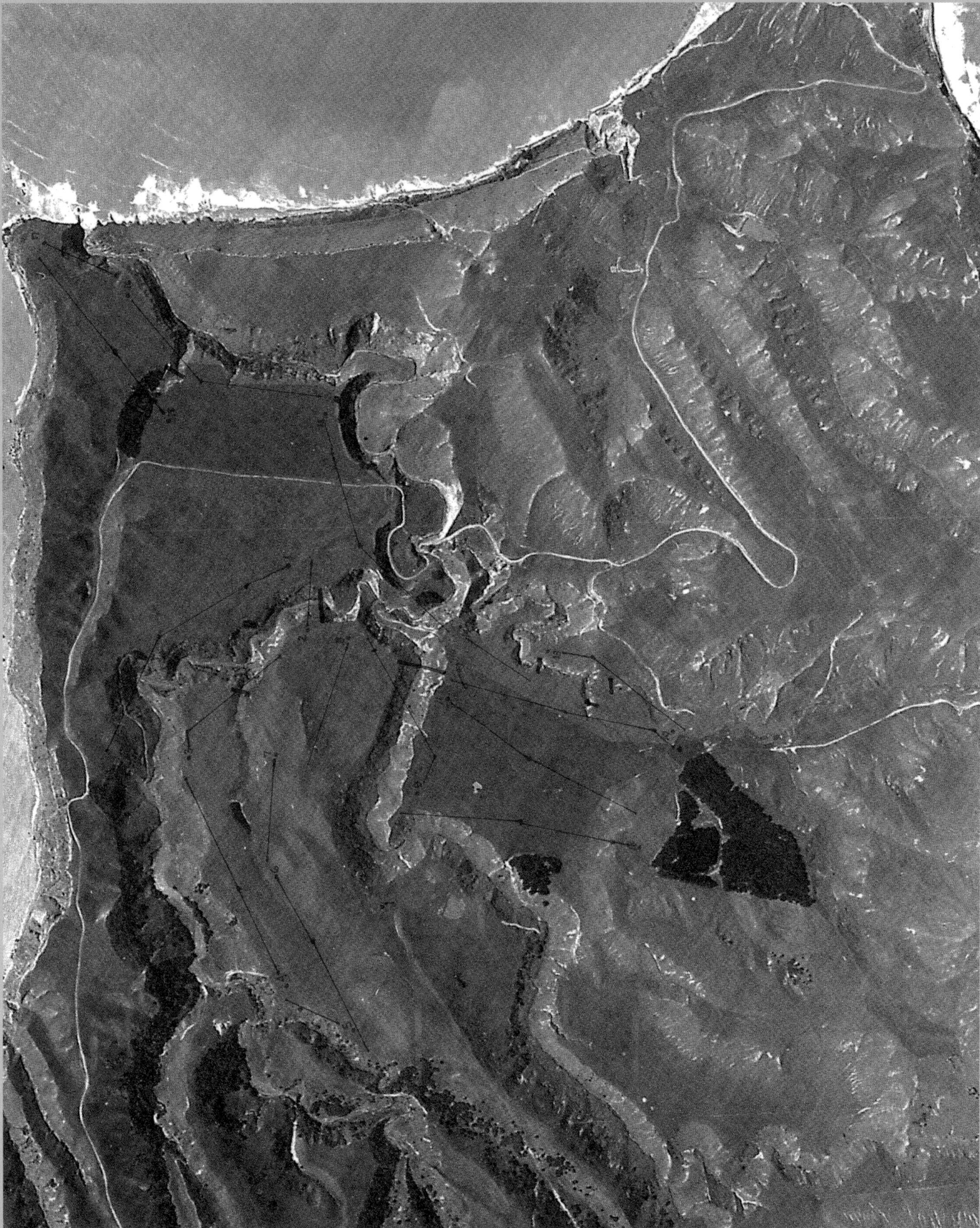

A possible routing plan for The Farm at Cape Kidnappers

Mid-round bridge traverse across the rapids of the Bijaypur River at the Himalayan Golf Course

The mind-bending Himalayan Golf Course, Nepal, with the stunning Annapurna range backdrop

When discussing would-be golf courses and the terrain they might occupy, comparisons always prove useful. Doak says he's seen pictures of the Los Angeles Country Club when George Thomas was there in the 1920s, laying out golf holes across and amid massive ravines. LACC back then (before every sort of development imaginable took shape around it) recalled The Farm in setting, Doak says – but not in scale. Doak believes we need to consult that brand-new Asia–Pacific top-100 to find another useful comp: #23, The Himalayan Golf Club in Pokhara, Nepal.

'You may not believe this place is worth the trip,' Doak says, playing tour guide again, 'especially when you're playing the first two holes – around a range that's netted in. But then you get down to No. 3, with the views of Annapurna, right there beside the [Bijaypur] river, crossing on bridges that are four feet above gushing water. Then you get it. It's just the kind of 'golf trek' we envisioned for The Farm.'

Yet neither comparison helps us appreciate The Farm's scale. Nor does aerial imagery. Through such a lens, what appears to be rows of hillocks are revealed to be small mountains when standing on site. I toured this property in April 2023: they are magnificent in the way they frame the lobes of golfing terrain, especially when they meet the coast then fall another seventy-five metres into the sea. The river valleys, up close? Full-on canyons up to one hundred feet deep. This shouldn't be *too* surprising: Cape Kidnappers may be famous for its massive cliffs but many of its inland holes are riven and flanked by similarly long, deep canyons that, on any other golf course, would stand out as the principal natural feature. Down on The Farm, however, those river canyons just happen to be the sticking point. Or they were, twenty years ago.

'We had initially envisioned a simple thing – an affordable course with just greens and tees, no irrigation – but the costs were never so simple. I had no idea what the bridges might cost; going over rivers down there, two of them, meant we needed three bridges of one hundred yards each, across the ravines. We finally got someone who knew that cost: a million US dollars per bridge!

'We were like, *Oh crap. This doesn't work quite so neatly now, knowing that*. There are roads that get you down and across those rivers, and you *could* play the course that way. Technically. But it's awkward. For example, you can get from the 2nd tee to the 2nd green by going all the way down and around, across the river and back up. But it's a long drive, much less a walk.'

The 15th green and 16th tee at Cape Kidnappers

Course architects are nothing if not problem-solvers. Listening to Doak talk about The Farm, it's clear the as-yet-disentangled conundrums associated with this project continue to nag at the man who brought us The Loop course in Michigan. On a theoretical level, the routing posed at The Farm has been solved, yet the practicalities associated with the bridge component continue to stump him.

'We've talked a lot about it over the years, in-house. Could we do it with fewer bridges? Well, you'd have to give up that 2nd through 8th hole lobe, or the 10 through 14 area, which is one of the coolest parts. Maybe it makes more sense as a nine-hole thing, not eighteen? ... We've also done one or two courses that were conceived as 'golf as a trek across cool ground' – meaning courses where the golf starts in one place and ends in another. But it's weird logistically. At Black Forest [in northern Michigan] we couldn't get it to work. At Dismal River [in western Nebraska], we did make it work, because we just didn't come back up such steep terrain from the river.'

At The Loop, Dismal River and dozens more projects, Doak managed to convince the client to take a chance and try something out of the box. After three decades in the business, Doak has become skilled at prosecuting these acts of persuasion, these sales puzzles. His failure to solve this one clearly disappoints him. 'Julian and I talked one more time about The Farm, but I never had the sense they were that serious about it. He was getting older and not seeing the appeal of this rough-and-ready thing we envisioned. Somehow, I never managed to convey just how good it would be.

'I've been spending so much time in New Zealand of late. It's hard not to think about The Farm. One thing I want to do someday is go back and build it.'

WHALSAY GOLFING: SCOTLAND'S MOST NORTHERLY ARCHIPELAGO

THE SHETLAND ISLANDS, SCOTLAND

WORDS AND PHOTOGRAPHY
BY CLYDE JOHNSON

LEFT
Looking back towards the 11th at Whalsay

The Shetland Islands sit at the northernmost edge of Britain, where the North Sea meets the Atlantic Ocean. Closer to Norway than to Edinburgh, this windswept archipelago of one hundred islands (only sixteen inhabited) is home to a surprising collection of golf courses, each with its own unique character shaped by the dramatic coastal landscape.

I had originally planned to take the thirteen-hour ferry from Aberdeen to reach the UK's most northerly archipelago, thinking this would be the more adventurous route. As it turns out, the flight from Edinburgh is just over an hour, including a brief touchdown in Kirkwall, the capital of the Orkney Isles. The Orkneys themselves, home to five golf courses and much closer to mainland Scotland, can wait for another trip – one with a more palatable ferry journey. Or perhaps a trip without my non-golfing (but very hospitable) wife!

After our brief stop in Kirkwall, our small plane – more of a flying bus, really – continues north, passing over Fair Isle far below. I think about its lighthouse keeper, who maintains what must be six of the most exposed golf holes imaginable, surrounded by the choppy waters of the North Sea. Soon we're landing at the southern tip of Shetland's mainland, where the precariously perched Sumburgh lighthouse provides an introduction to the island's rugged isolation. The journey from here is inevitably north, but not before we stop to mosey around Old Scatness Broch, an Iron Age village that lay undiscovered for over a millennium. Shetland has a rich heritage and a culture that blends pre-1472 links to Norway and the Vikings with its relatively contemporaneous ties to Scotland.

While there's one main road to the capital, Lerwick (pronounced 'Ler-ick'), it's worth taking the detours. Just a few miles off the main route, the west coast of Shetland's narrow southern tail reveals its rewards. Here we find the largest tombolo (a beach connecting two pieces of land, for those less geographically minded) leading to St Ninian's Isle. It's a picturesque spot, peaceful even in peak season. Further north on the island of Yell, friendly Shetland ponies roam the beaches. These side trips also introduce us to the charming character of island life – local produce sold via the honour system from the most inventive storage solutions: eggs tucked in old microwaves, cookies left in bus-stop libraries and homemade cakes chilling in roadside fridges.

About half of Shetland's population lives within ten miles of Lerwick. We found the sweet spot for accommodation just on the edge of this zone – close enough to access the mainland's three golf courses, but far enough out to experience both the convenience of town and the charm of remote island life.

The Shetland Golf Club dates to the oil boom of the 1970s. That explains the surprisingly good quality of the road infrastructure, which far exceeds that of Scotland's Western Isles (and most of the mainland!). The course is nestled in a beautiful valley overlooking Dales Voe – a long, narrow sea inlet typical of Shetland's coastline (the word 'voe' comes from the Norse for 'bay' or 'fjord', a reminder of the islands' Viking heritage).The start is a beauty, tracking down and across the western slope of the valley towards the upper reaches of this Atlantic sea loch. Play is soon switched to the easterly slope, after a par-4 hops a ditch and the Burn of Dale that runs along the base of the valley and splits the course. This switch will happen several times throughout the round, but the most dramatic use of the burn is tackled early on. The 5th angles across the Burn of Dale with a long approach, and then heading back upstream the 6th tracks and then jumps over the babbling water to a skinny bank.

It's an unsophisticated assault up to and down from the clubhouse at the 7th and 10th, but it does allow for an out-and-back over the valley's more harshly slanted west side. Here, the ever-present burn shadows the 11th hole before the course climbs again, this time via a par-3, which edges upward to where the island's main road horseshoes around the valley top. While the routing thoughtfully distributes its features throughout, there are moments where necessity trumps elegance – like the severely benched 13th green carved into the eastern heights. The short-four 16th teases an angled drive over heather, as the layout switches for the final time. With a bluntly upward par-3, and then an awkwardly hitching approach to the par-5 18th, the finish stutters home.

Even with those near-endless summer evenings, shadows are cast over The Dale earlier than you would want or expect, such is the steepness of the enveloping slopes. So I waited until the following morning to tackle that second nine.

A few miles east, the fertile Tingwall Valley offers a gentler landscape than The Dale's rugged terrain. Here lies Asta Golf Course, where ten holes are nestled where two lochs meet. Or rather, eighteen holes – the course switches between two different nine-hole layouts on a bi-weekly basis. Between water and road, a lumpy spine splits the centre of the property, bringing the odd moment of funky intrigue. My visit coincided with the 'New' nine.

The New routing heads clockwise, with its second hole carrying back over the corner of the lake before finishing with a blind par-3. The classic layout takes a more direct path south. Both routings feature long holes that track alongside the lochs, where clouds of midges – Scotland's infamous tiny biting flies – add an extra challenge. While the middle stretch of both layouts offers less tactical variety, the simply slanted greens provide plenty of entertainment, especially when viewed against the deep blue water and mottled purple heather of the surrounds. The best hole – a fifty-eight-yard semi-blind dip to the loch shore – was reserved for the classic nine – not that it stopped me from playing it!

Asta Golf Course

The opening hole at Whalsay

Whalsay Golf Club

Until 2018, maps of Scotland typically showed the Shetland Islands in a separate box, disconnected from the mainland. This cartographic quirk has been banned, forcing mapmakers to show just how far north these islands really stretch. Even more remote is the island of Unst, reached by two ferry journeys from Shetland's mainland. At its northern tip, the Hermaness National Nature Reserve marks the end of the British Isles, offering spectacular displays of seabird acrobatics.

The tourist board claims golfers still play among the dunes at nearby Burrafirth, though evidence of this is hard to find. More certain is the history of the Royal Air Force's nine-hole course at the now-closed Saxa Vord base. Built in the 1960s, this clifftop track wove through dramatic gulleys and was famous for hosting twenty-four-hour matches during the endless summer days.

Today, Whalsay Golf Club claims the title of Britain's most northerly course – and surely its most beautiful. Just 300 miles south of the Arctic Circle but accessible by a mere thirty-minute ferry ride, Whalsay was the true purpose of my journey north. Rarely does a dream destination align with perfect conditions, but today delivers cloudless skies, calm winds and the endless light of near-solstice.

From the main town of Symbister's busy harbour (although busy and even 'town' should be taken in context), a ten-minute drive traces the rugged coastline before climbing to reveal an impossibly glassy ocean below. The clubhouse could be any of Scotland's modest sporting hubs, with a charming short course nestled between it and the water. Twenty-five pounds into the honesty box seems a bargain – I would have paid anything for what lay ahead.

The opening hole sets the tone for what's to come: a par-4 that banks down and around the coastline onto a dramatic peninsula devoted entirely to golf. By the time you reach the long 3rd hole, you're nearly at the headland's tip. The 4th drives thrillingly across a rocky bay before climbing back towards what locals call the Skaw – an Old Norse word for promontory that appears frequently on Shetland maps. This natural ridge creates a spine through the course, reaching its crescendo at the 9th hole.

The holes playing away from the cliff edges might be less dramatic, but they're no less captivating. What's particularly striking is the quality of the greens – immaculately maintained despite the harsh coastal environment. Perhaps this shouldn't be surprising; the island's population of 1,000 supports a thriving fishing industry, and clearly some of that prosperity has found its way to the golf course.

The back nine opens by crossing to the far side of the island – and seemingly to the edge of the world. The par-5 10th demands a blind drive along the waves before finding its green craftily angled behind a quaint loch. Shortly after, you reach the furthest point of land, where the course makes a dramatic ninety-degree turn along the coast, forcing you to negotiate an unexpectedly deep inlet. This stretch, pushing towards the island's interior, proves even more engaging than the front nine. The 13th, fronted by a water-filled trench, is followed by a gorgeous par-3 where twin shoulders of land melt elegantly into the green.

Shetland Golf Club

The Knab

Then comes a sequence of holes that edge ever closer to the brink. Nothing prepares you for the scene at the 16th tee: sheep grazing peacefully in the foreground belie the drama ahead, as your drive must carry a carved-out nook in the cliff face. The fairway sweeps and slants towards its jagged edge, while the green sits impossibly wrapped behind a gaping inlet. Beyond lies nothing but untouched expanse. After an inevitable climb, the course offers one final thrill – a chance to drive aggressively from on high as the closing hole bends determinedly around a loch.

Our golfing journey concludes back in Lerwick at The Knab, a headland jutting into Breiwick Bay, where someone has ingeniously squeezed nine short holes onto the sloping clifftops. It's free to play and, aside from local dog walkers, you'll have the place to yourself. The official routing – if you choose to follow it – sees the 2nd hole climb to a coastguard station before the 3rd angles beyond a ditch along the heights. Housing borders the course until the 6th, which steps up to the far side of the lookout. On a clear day, the views would be infinite, especially from the elevated 7th tee. The closing holes track precariously along the cliff's edge, the crashing waves far below a constant reminder of the setting. Time your visit right and you might find freshly mowed greens, but either way, this quirky course offers a fitting end to a Shetland golf adventure.

Our final day is spent in the harbour town of Scalloway, wilfully ignoring warnings about flight cancellations. The band of fog that had settled over the island's southern reaches would indeed ground all planes that day. That overnight ferry might have been the wiser choice, but thanks to the incredible hospitality of some locals, our extended stay merely added to the charm of this remarkable archipelago.

SAND, SOIL AND SEOUL: NOTES FROM THE ROAD

WORDS AND PHOTOGRAPHY
BY LUKAS MICHEL

'A highlight of my day? A 245-yard ace on the 11th with my 4-wood.'

Five weeks, three continents, one hole-in-one. As Lukas Michel travels from LA's classics to Korea's extravagance, his road diary offers a rare insight from the dual perspective of course architect and accomplished amateur. Each fairway walked reveals not just the game, but the design philosophy that shapes it.

Day 1 – The Bear

My bags packed, I bid farewell to my girlfriend, who had been incredibly supportive through all my work-related travel, and hopped into an Uber to Melbourne Airport.

The airport routine went smoothly, and we departed on time. I'd preloaded *The Bear* onto my iPad and found unexpected parallels between a chef's life and my role as a golf course architect. A particular quote stuck with me: *'Most of the incredible things I've eaten haven't been because the skill level is exceptionally high ... it's because it's been really inspired.'* That perspective resonated deeply and motivated me to stay open-minded for all I will experience in the world of course design.

Day 2 – Taco Tuesday

Landing in Los Angeles brings the usual mix of jet lag and wanderlust. A continental roll from a local deli in El Segundo was my introduction to the area, savoured on a park bench amid the hum of unfamiliar surroundings.

Day 3 – Wilshire

A solid nine hours of sleep successfully reset my internal clock. A friend picked me up for a catch-up at Los Angeles Country Club, where we shared breakfast, traded stories and tweaked his game over a casual range session.

The main event was Wilshire Country Club, my first Norman MacBeth course, set for an upcoming Kyle Phillips renovation. The intimate routing and frequent changes of direction led to an extremely memorable course. It highlighted the importance of doing everything possible to make each hole distinct, inherently improving the variety and memorability of the course. The day closed with dinner on the clubhouse veranda with my playing partners, a typically spectacular Los Angeles sunset adding to the ambiance.

Day 4 – Bel-Air

The day began with a jolt – a 4.8 magnitude earthquake that had me contemplating the structural integrity of Bel-Air Country Club's famous tunnels before my round. A morning coffee with Geoff Shackelford proved insightful and full of candid takes on the world of golf. Topics included PGA/LIV, course renovations and USGA greens construction methods.

At Bel-Air, I joined a fascinating group that included Andy Johnson and the course superintendent. The round was a mix of quirky incidents (our member host nearly hitting the same person twice) and debates on various topics (including an extended one about the property's highest point, which doesn't pass the eye test), all played on a superb, firm and fast course. The conditions fully realised George Thomas's design, allowing his crafty features to come to life (most notably the approaches into 1, 4, 8, 10, 12, 13 and 15). The majority of these features allow a running approach to work towards the green with a correct shot shape or angle, but complicate play otherwise.

Andy and I capped off the day with a shared Uber, discussing new developments and trends in modern course architecture.

Day 5 – Heading South

Travel days have their own charm – or chaos. After a delayed flight from Los Angeles to Atlanta, I commenced my three-hour drive to Aiken, South Carolina at 7 pm.

Day 6 – The Ace

Gravel roads led to the strikingly unique Old Barnwell. The immediate impression was a handmade feel, with features seemingly raked and shovelled by hand rather than the typical heavy machinery of modern design.

The course tumbles its way through ideal golfing ground, from a high plateau early, across and down into some lower ground, before crescendoing to a finish. It's a great way to explore the property and thus a great routing. But what has stuck with me is the course's bold and ornamental personality, which has left me curious about how it will age.

A highlight of my day? A 245-yard ace on the 11th with my 4-wood.

After some work at my Airbnb, I met friend and host, Morgan, for dinner in Aiken, closing the day with stories from the building of the course.

Day 7 – Palmetto

The morning was quiet, spent catching up on some design work. After lunch, it was off to Palmetto Golf Club, where Morgan's a member. We zipped around the course in a cart, revisiting its MacKenzie-influenced bold shaping. It's unclear exactly how long The Doctor spent here, but what is clear is that a lot of Palmetto's character is derived from those visits.

Day 8 – Tree Farm and Broomsedge

The first of a two-course day is Tree Farm, graciously accompanied by head pro, Drew King. The course felt mature despite its youth, blending seamlessly into its landscape – a design style aligned closely with my personal tastes. I loved the par-3 opening hole (with shades of St George's Hill's 8th) but standout moments to me were the intimate short par-4 6th, the treacherous 9th green, the bold 12th green and approach, the doglegging 13th, the grand redan 15th and the enticing short par-4 18th. If Old Barnwell, with its exotic and spicy features, is Thai cuisine, Tree Farm has the delicacy and refinement of French fare.

Next stop: a pre-opening walk around Broomsedge, Mike Koprowski's passion project. The course is compact yet bursting with character. Highlights included the beautifully bunkered par-3 5th, the postage-stamp 11th and the muscular green site at the 12th. As rain approached, my pace quickened, though this didn't stop me pausing countless times on my way in to soak up the bold design. I look forward to returning to play to see how the place compares to its nearby modern competitors.

Day 9 – Pinehurst's No. 10

After a light workout at Anytime Fitness, I grabbed lunch at Five Guys and headed to Pinehurst's No. 10.

The course was in stunning shape. The native areas were particularly impressive, helping soften the edge from artificial to natural. I found it a perfect blend of walkability, interesting shots and aesthetic charm. The brawny 6th green sticks in my mind, as well as the tumbling 8th fairway, the perfectly framed 9th tee shot, the difficult long par-3 14th and the cascading 17th green.

On top of that, Pinehurst nailed every detail, from scorecards to course furniture, enhancing the experience.

Day 10 – Southern Pines and Kinloch

Donald Ross's Southern Pines dazzled in the dew and morning light. I walked the course clubless with Ran Morrissett, soaking in the morning rays and Kyle Franz's mature restoration work. This might be the best property in the area for golf, with more undulating drama than the famous No. 2 course, but without the heaving and severe slopes some others like Pine Needles or Mid Pines. Another one to return to play on a future visit.

After lunch with Ran and a coffee for the road, a rainy drive north led me to Kinloch. Practice facilities here were stellar, and I spent the afternoon honing my game ahead of the tournament.

Will Davenport – fellow Mid-Am competitor, and my caddie in my 2019 victory – arrived late from Florida.

Day 11 – Kinloch Practice

Will was groggy from his late arrival, and an even later work call, so I joined his friends for a morning round at Kinloch. We played a casual skins match on the back nine – my game felt sharp, though I ended up five dollars down after a few halved birdies.

In the afternoon, I spent time refining my short game, which felt rusty after months spent more often on bulldozers than with my clubs.

Kinloch was pleasant but, unlike some of the courses I'd seen on this trip so far, it didn't align with my design preferences. Holes 15 to 17 (6 to 8 in the Mid-Am routing) stood out as a brilliant and drama-inducing stretch for tournament golf.

Day 12 – Independence Practice

The second course for stroke play, Independence Golf Club, offered a slightly wilder ride. One hole of note (not necessarily good), the 12th, demanded precision – 220 metres to carry a hazard, with a fifty-metre-wide fairway squeezed between red stakes on both sides. Overall, I was impressed by the raised greens and shorter cut surrounds, which created a variety of recovery shots and – in this respect – more interesting golf than at Kinloch.

My group included Mike McCoy, the 2013 Mid-Am champion, in his final exempt year. Watching him navigate a fairly long and difficult course was a pleasure.

Post-round, I felt quite confident in my game, though I knew with months out of touch with competitive golf, the tournament would test me.

Day 13 – Tournament Round 1: Independence

The opening round at Independence was a steady start. A 1-over-par round kept me in contention, despite two errant drives on the 8th and 18th holes that I miraculously saved for pars.

It was a relief not to throw away the tournament on day one, a mistake I'd made in 2022 at Erin Hills.

Day 14 – Tournament Round 2: Kinloch

The day started strong with two birdies on my opening nine, but a rough patch on the back nine derailed my momentum. Several bogeys, including a missed four-footer on the penultimate hole, and another on the difficult last left me just outside the matchplay cut.

It was frustrating to miss the mark after flying halfway across the world, but the silver lining was that my overall game felt better than in previous years. I found some solace in cheering Will on as he nailed his final putt to secure his spot in matchplay.

Day 15 – Exploring DC

A two-hour drive to Washington DC gave me time to decompress, and I spent the afternoon exploring the city.

Day 16 – A DC Golf Odyssey

The day was packed with golf course visits. First, I checked out Chevy Chase Club, where superintendent Stephen Britton was managing a renovation with Andrew Green.

Chatting with Stephen, an interesting topic was broached – when to restore and when to renovate? Chevy Chase was arguably its best in the 1920s and 1930s; however, all evidence points to it just being good and never great. Given the minimal difference in cost between renovating and restoring, the club chose to pursue a more aggressive plan. I look forward to seeing how this pays off.

Next, it was a quick cart tour of Burning Tree, one of the town's most private clubs, and where Gil Hanse had done some work.

Finally, we headed to Congressional, chaperoned by Stephen and their superintendent. Andrew Green's bold renovation work shone, although I left curious to see the pros' reactions to it at the 2030 PGA.

Driving back to my friend's place, I was brimming with enthusiasm for the design work I'd seen, and keen to return to play all three courses at some point.

Day 17 – Bidermann

More highway driving from Washington DC to Wilmington, Delaware, brought me to Bidermann Golf Club. My host had assembled a competitive group, and we played a fun match at a club that blended exclusivity with unpretentious charm. I could see semblance of my home club, Metropolitan, in the design, the link being the architect, Dick Wilson, who designed both in the 1960s. Wilson had a predilection to two things: well-bunkered doglegs and booze. Bidermann had great examples of the former, a standout being the 18th.

Day 18 – The Witch

After a long drive to Connecticut, I arrived just in time for a practice round at Stanwich Club for The Farrell, a rising Mid-Am event. The course impressed with its impeccable conditioning, thoughtful layout and even better logo (a witch riding a flagstick). Notable holes included the cross-slope short par-4 3rd, the diabolical par-3 8th (soon to be rebuilt by OCM), the downhill and dogleg left 10th, and the a-little-too-severe postage stamp 16th (also soon going under the knife), which round out an engaging and interesting tournament test. Hopefully OCM take some edge off the 8th and 16th without distorting their character too much.

Day 19 – Farrell Round 1

My driver was dialled in today, threading the tight fairways of Stanwich. The putter, normally my strength, was a little cold.

Eventually, the tide turned and I holed some putts just as my driving faltered. I seeded fifth of sixteen for matchplay.

Day 20 – Matchplay Double-header

The morning match pitted me against a seasoned New York State Amateur champ. It was a tight battle, but a few late mistakes on his part secured my win on the 17th.

The afternoon match was equally tense. My opponent, John, was backed by a boisterous caddie whose antics toed the line of distraction. While amusing, it seemed to rattle John more than me. I closed the match on the iconic 16th, winning 3/2.

Exhausted but exhilarated, I prepared for the semi-final, knowing tough tests lay ahead.

Day 21 – Semi-final Showdown

I faced Christian Cavaliere in the semi-final. Christian had qualified for the 2023 US Open, barely missing the cut. It was a mix of great and scrappy golf from both sides.

A highlight of my round was a twenty-five-foot eagle putt on the 14th that got me back to one down, but Christian's consistency edged me out. I lost 2/1, ending a good run of golf on a style of golf I have typically struggled on.

My friend Will also bowed out in his semi-final. We commiserated over drinks before he jetted off on an earlier-than-hoped flight. I packed for my next adventure: Japan and Korea.

Day 22 – Hello, Japan

A red-eye flight from JFK to Haneda (including some beautiful but impossible-to-photograph aurora over the North Pole) got me into Tokyo early Tuesday morning. By 7:30 am, I was on the 1st tee at Taiheiyo Gotemba, shaking off jet lag with a practice round.

The course was solid and typically Japanese, with tight fairways bordered by dense trees, and thick korai grass rough. Recent bunker work by Rees Jones (and led by Quinn Thompson, a well-known shaper) furnished the greens and fairways beautifully, but the course still lacked a routing that took advantage of the site well (namely, not a single hole aligns to iconic Mount Fuji).

Day 23 – Slow Practice

Practice day two began with a shotgun start at 9 am. An overcrowded course led to a frustratingly slow pace of play. Stubbornness kept me from walking off, but after three hours for the front nine, I wondered if I should have.

The evening brought a reprieve: the tournament reception at Fuji Speedway. Standing on the iconic track's home straight, surreal moments from my Gran Turismo childhood came to life. Mingling, entertainment (including sumo wrestlers) and great food rounded out the day.

Day 24 – Tournament Round 1

I started on the 10th and played a solid opening stretch, highlighted by a birdie on the par-3 13th. A tree-related double bogey at the 15th was frustrating, but I recovered with a birdie at the 18th to turn at even par.

My back nine was a rollercoaster: a chip-in birdie at the 2nd and a gutsy up-and-down at the 3rd offset weak bogeys on the 4th and 8th. I finished with a respectable 1-over-par.

The afternoon was spent practising before retreating to my hotel, where the clouds rolled in to ominously obscure Mount Fuji.

Day 25 – Rain and Ramen

Rain and fog delayed my second round, eventually postponing it entirely.

Day 26 – Marathon Golf

The weather cleared, and the tournament organisers were determined to squeeze in as much golf as possible. I started early, tackling Round 2 on a soft, rain-soaked course. My struggles from the previous day carried over – I scraped through nine holes at 3-over, and things didn't improve on the back. A disappointing seventy-six put me out of contention, but I made the cut.

After a quick break, Round 3 began. My play remained inconsistent, though I managed a small victory: sinking a birdie in darkness on my 6th hole just as play was suspended.

Day 27 – The Final Stretch

The tournament's conclusion was a slog through two rounds of uninspired golf. My morning started positively with a birdie on my par-3 8th, but a series of bogeys left me with a seventy-three. By the afternoon, the grind took its toll. My seventy-four was a collection of small mistakes, though a few well-earned birdies kept it respectable.

Standing behind the 18th green as the tournament concluded, I reflected on the talent in this field. Players like Wenyi Ding, who may well become a star, reminded me of how good one needs to be to reach the top of this game. It was humbling and validating that I'd chosen the right path, away from competitive golf.

Day 28 – Business in Tokyo

With the tournament behind me, I headed to Tokyo for a business meeting before catching the Shinkansen to the Izu Peninsula, and Kawana Golf Resort.

Kawana's hotel and course exuded history and character. I explored a few holes at dusk, the coastal view living up to its 'Pebble Beach of Japan' reputation.

Day 29 – Kawana Magic

I played Kawana in the morning, starting with a spectacular thirty-metre drop off the 1st tee. The routing made the most of the hilly, oceanfront terrain, with highlights like the short par-4 7th, where rumpled fairways framed a knoll-top green.

Kawana is an incredible candidate for a restoration. Unfortunately, another parallel with Pebble Beach is this would be almost impossible. Closing the course for an extended period would lose so much revenue on a course that is extremely busy. Hopefully, one day something will happen, but my hopes aren't very high.

That afternoon, I returned to Tokyo and checked into a compact but comfortable hotel in Akasaka.

Day 30 – A Tourist in Tokyo

The day began with Japanese-style pancakes before a guest appearance on a friend's podcast, The Tie. We chatted about my travels, the courses I'd seen and what lay ahead.

After a tonkatsu lunch, I headed to Shinjuku to witness the bustling street crossings while browsing some modern golf fashion offered a moment of calm amid the chaos of Tokyo.

Day 31 – Seoul Arrival

My morning flight brought me to Seoul, where I checked into the luxurious Josun Palace Hotel in the Gangnam District. The international team for the Bridges Cup gathered for a walking food tour led by our Korean host, Jun. It was an excellent introduction to both Seoul and my teammates, many who I'd not met. The stage was set for a fantastic week ahead.

Day 32 – Jeju Island Blitz

A 4:30 am alarm signalled the start of a whirlwind day. After a hectic airport security experience involving a rogue rangefinder battery, we caught the world's busiest air route to Jeju Island. We headed straight to Nine Bridges Golf Club. The modern design was scenic and thoughtful, though not entirely my style. Waterfalls, dramatic bunkers and large greens offered a pleasant and polished experience.

One hole that did stand out to me – likely due to its restraint, relying on contour and not bunkering and rough – was the 8th on the creek nine. Its infinity green reminded me of the 17th at Crystal Downs or the 7th at Kawana, from just days earlier.

Day 33 – Practice at Haesley

A relaxed breakfast was highlighted by the hotel's dim sum bar before we set out to Haesley Nine Bridges, the tournament venue.

Arriving at the course, the clubhouse and accommodation were the first to impress. The clubhouse is adorned with high ceilings supported by intricate timber work, an architectural masterpiece to behold.

My playing partner, Jacob, and I then headed for the course, with a light-hearted practice round, though the pace of play slowed as we trailed behind Korean legend K J Choi giving lessons. We won our friendly match, buoyed by a stunning ace by one of our teammates on the 220-metre 17th hole.

The course, much like Nine Bridges, is a display of design and construction extravagance. Although not my flavour, there is plenty of inspiration and lessons to take away, one of which is fitting good golf on a severe site. The 16th hole plays across a severe hillside, and incredible amounts of earth must have been moved to make this hole playable. But it's a standout and I'm glad to be able to experience the end product, as the rock wall water features are executed beautifully and the views down below are stunning. It's not something I may have tried, but it's something I'd look to doing with the necessary budget in the future.

Day 34 – Media Day

The morning was filled with media obligations – photos, interviews and official duties – before a second practice round. Partnering with Nick, the team's ace-maker, we tested alternative pairings while enjoying another fun round.

Day 35 – Bridges Cup Day 1

The morning's four-ball matches started strong for Jacob and me. We took an early lead and closed out a solid 3/2 win, though the rest of the team struggled, leaving us down 1–5 overall.

Lunch was a quick break in one of the three incredible halfway houses before afternoon foursomes. It was a tight match early, but birdies on 13 and 14 helped to seal a 4/3 victory. The team rallied to win the session 3–1, narrowing the gap to 4–6 by the end of the day.

Day 36 – Bridges Cup Day 2

In the morning foursomes, Jacob and I maintained our momentum, grinding out a 2/1 win against a strong pairing. The team battled hard across the board, splitting the morning session 3–3. The overall score tightened to 7–9, with everything to play for in the afternoon four-ball.

Our next opponents were formidable, and we knew we'd need something special. Jacob shone with brilliant birdies at 5, 9 and 10. On the 11th, after I left him in the rough, he hit a towering 3-wood from 220 metres, landing just twelve feet away. It was one of the best shots of the tournament.

A clutch birdie putt from me on 14 took us to three up, but a nervy moment arose on the 16th. Faced with a tough decision from 210 metres over water, I opted for an aggressive shot ... and pulled it into the hazard. Our opponents capitalised, and the momentum shifted.

By the 17th, darkness was setting in. I hit another poor shot and we were standing just one up on the 18th tee. Jacob's drive found trouble right, leaving us scrambling. Our opponents were safe but not good in the right rough. Somehow, I produced a high-cut 5-iron to just short of the green, a minor miracle under the circumstances.

The US team called play due to the fading light and the match was left suspended. Tension simmered as we headed into dinner, knowing the outcome of the match would hinge on a few minutes of play tomorrow morning.

Day 37 – The Final Day

Jacob practised shots to replicate his upcoming scenario on the 18th green. His initial attempts were inconsistent, but some quick adjustment sharpened his touch. By the time we headed to the course, he was dialled in.

Our opponents restarted play from a tricky lie. They missed, left in the water, putting the balance of outcomes in our favour. They overshot the green after their drop, leaving Jacob to execute a smooth bump-and-run to ten feet, enough for us to secure the win. The session was a mix of results, with the international team splitting the matches 2–2. The score stood at 9–11.

In singles, I faced Tug Maude, whom Jacob and I had just battled. My game was sharp, and I built a commanding 4-up lead through nine. Tug rallied, sinking birdies on 12 and 13 to close the gap. Standing on the 16th fairway, I was faced with a shot nearly identical to my misstep the night before. This time, I committed fully to a 5-iron, striking it perfectly onto the green. Two steady putts secured the hole, taking me back to two up. On the 17th, a daunting 245-metre par-3, I struck my 4-wood flush. It landed six feet from the pin, and Tug conceded the match. The win capped off an undefeated performance for the week, and I felt proud of my contribution as the team's fate hung in the balance.

The deciding match came down to Angus Carrick and Joe Deraney, tied heading to the 18th green. Both hit superb approach shots, leaving eight- and ten-foot birdie putts. Angus lined his up, and it looked destined to drop ... but it lipped out. Joe stepped up, rolling his in for the win. The Americans celebrated, having edged us out 17–15.

There was heartbreak in our camp, but we applauded the effort. On the bus ride back to Seoul, the team lightened the mood with beers and banter, the camaraderie softening the sting of coming so close.

Day 38 – Homeward Bound

I woke feeling rested, albeit slightly hungover. A buffet breakfast at the Josun Palace revived me, and I enjoyed one last Starbucks Reserve coffee with the assistant captain before packing up for the journey home.

As I sat on the tarmac, awaiting my flight home, I reflected on the past five-and-a-half weeks. The trip had been a whirlwind – new courses, unforgettable experiences and incredible people.

Though the loss at the Bridges Cup lingered, it was overshadowed by the gratitude I felt for the opportunity to compete, explore and spend time with fantastic people.

TE ARAI LINKS

AUCKLAND & MANGAWHAI, NEW ZEALAND

WORDS & PHOTOGRAPHY
BY WILLIAM WATT

LEFT
High above Te Arai Links South Course

Whether helicoptering amid Bond-esque luxury or commandeering a targeted red-eye mission, determination pays off when I finally capture magic hour's radiance washing over Te Arai Links' sublime Coore & Crenshaw design. A third trip saw the superb North Course added to the itinerary, bringing Te Arai Links firmly into view as one of the world's greatest golf destinations.

There's a wonderful Italian expression called '*sprezzatura*'. It refers to 'a certain nonchalance, so as to conceal all art and make whatever one does or says appear to be without effort and almost without any thought about it.' *Sprezzatura* can be applied to many personal as well as professional settings, and golf is a great outlet to explore this state. Is there anything more demoralising to an opponent than getting up and down from a deep greenside bunker, or hitting yet another five-footer to win the match? Both are skills that require hours of unseen practice to master, yet when executed out on course, can appear effortless (provided you pair it with a nonchalant celebration).

This story took three full attempts, six flights (two red-eyes), six cars, a boat, a helicopter and eighteen months to complete. The three trips couldn't have been more different, though all were beautiful in their own way.

Attempt One – The (Almost) Ultimate Luxury Trip

After a relaxing afternoon flight from Melbourne to Auckland, I am picked up at the airport in a black BMW 7-Series and whisked into the city for my single night stay at The Hotel Britomart. For those with design and architecture sensibilities, The Britomart is the place to stay in Auckland; it's one of those rare experiences that combine warmth and comfort with an edgy cool.

After a restful night in one of the most comfortable beds I've ever experienced, lunch on Waiheke Island beckons, a short ferry trip away. Despite being within view of the city skyline, the atmosphere on Waiheke feels a million miles away. Quiet, serene and a little bohemian, the locals here seem to know they're onto a good thing.

Waiheke is home to around 10,000 residents and has become a popular destination for Aucklanders looking for an easy weekend away, or even a day trip to one of the wineries that dot the island. One of the most popular is Mudbrick Vineyard and Restaurant, set in an expansive rustic farmhouse high on the hill, with stunning views across the water to Auckland city. As with everything I've eaten since touching down, lunch here is superb.

After lunch, it's a short trek to the highest point on the property (and one of the highest on Waiheke) to the waiting black helicopter that will be zipping me up the coast to Te Arai in around half an hour. The drive to Te Arai Links from Auckland is not an arduous one (ninety minutes direct), but it's hard to top the unspoilt views, speed and, let's face it, sheer fun of taking a chopper.

One exception might be the tranquil surrounds of Mangawhai and Te Arai Links itself, but as we descend on the ribbons of bright green turf weaving through pristine white sand dunes and pine forest, my heart starts pumping a little faster. As the struts of the helicopter touch down gently on the ultra-fine fescue landing pad at the end of the driving range, a black van pulls up, ready to take me to my accommodation. The feeling of being on property is serene – everything is pared back, minimalist and exudes quality. If a singular physical place could define *sprezzatura*, then this must surely be it.

LEFT Te Arai Links South Course (foreground) and North Course (top)

Check-in is completed in the serene, ultra-minimalist clubhouse and as I roll up to the similarly subdued accommodation pods, I notice something that quietly blows my mind. As someone who spends a good chunk of my working life in a golf cart, I've had more than my share of spilled drinks, dropped cameras and crushed sunglasses from the bumps and shakes translated from the uneven ground of golf courses and resorts. But at Te Arai Links, there are absolutely no gutters. Every threshold, from the clubhouse to the driving range to the car park to the accommodation, is completely flush. It sounds like a simple thing, but as the husband of an architect, I know how difficult this is to achieve, even on the scale of residential buildings. To have no visible guttering or thresholds on a commercial scale shows an attention to detail that is rare. And it doesn't stop there; the services for each of the accommodation pods – heating, air conditioning, laundry and disposal facilities – are discreetly hidden in separate but matching pods, offering no distraction from the beautifully calm timber cladding and natural landscaping.

That natural, relaxed feeling continues as I enter the deluxe accommodation. There's nothing showy or flashy about it, just all very high quality. A private balcony overlooking the 1st fairway of the South Course, with a veiled view of the ocean beyond through a line of pine trees, tops it off.

But that's where the smooth sailing, the duck above water vibes, ends. What follows this jaw-dropping arrival is three days of unseasonably poor weather. It turns out in this part of the world, the arrival of La Niña means northern New Zealand briefly resembles northern Scotland – constant driving rain and gale-force winds that bend the surrounding pine trees over like giant flagsticks (which were also bending over).

I keep hoping for just a small break in the weather to photograph the course in something resembling the typically perfect climate in these parts. It never comes. Having come this far, I decide to battle out a solo eighteen holes on the South Course in the driving rain and, somewhat to my amazement – although I should know better having played a few Coore & Crenshaw masterpieces in my time – the course remains extremely playable. In fact, I somehow end up enjoying the sodden walk and embracing the contours of the routing through a forced ground game. The satisfaction of putting out on eighteen, having only lost one ball and logging what for me is a very tidy eighty, was immense. After a hot shower and a couple of warming ales at Ric's, I'm able to enjoy the sort of relaxation only a photographer can know. Horrible conditions equals time to put up your feet. It's a blessing and a curse – whenever fine weather appears, there is an immediate feeling of pressure to go and shoot. Even sitting at home with no particular job on, if a beautiful sunset is brewing, I'll want to be out there.

I do get out on course for a few photography sessions, and am able to capture some solid player's perspective shots of the course. And I'm enjoying experimenting with film, running some Kodak Gold 35 mm through. But in the back of my mind, I know I'll need to return. And that's a nice thought to have as I'm picked up in a private car and whisked back to Auckland. As we take off homeward bound for Melbourne and break through the clouds, I see the sun for the first time since getting on the chopper on Waiheke Island. Hopefully, next time, it will shine a little on the golf course and beautiful landscapes of Te Arai Links.

The Ocean Restaurant overlooks the 18th green of the South Course.

Attempt Two – The Sniper Mission

The weather in our part of the world moves almost exclusively from west to east. This means whatever conditions we are experiencing in south-eastern Australia are likely to be similar 'across the ditch' in New Zealand a couple of days later. But even with this cheat code in place, trying to time the weather for an international trip is purely a matter of playing the odds: nothing is certain and at some point, you've got to just pull the trigger and go. And so I'm on a red-eye flight from Melbourne to Auckland, back for another attempt to capture Te Arai Links in better light. It's been almost six months since my last visit, but the planning for this trip has been a lot more streamlined – no relaxing stay in Auckland, no fancy dinners and winery lunches, and definitely no luxury helicopter transfers. This is a purely tactical, special operations-style mission: return with a strong album of photography and video from Te Arai Links, or die.

It doesn't take long until I'm missing the creature comforts of my last trip. Since my last visit, Auckland (and large parts of Auckland Airport) have experienced once-in-a-generation floods, and the long trek to the temporary hire car facilities means I'm feeling all 45 kilograms of my luggage. Despite it being 2:30 am and being literally the only person at Auckland Airport collecting a car, the process seems to be taking an age. By the time I roll out of the car park, it's after 3 am and I'm already battling with Google Maps – the route it is suggesting doesn't seem very 'tactical' and looks to involve a bunch of rural roads that I don't really fancy battling at this time of night. I drag the route back onto State Highway 1 (SH1), the main road artery of New Zealand that runs literally the length of the country, and get going.

The par-3 17th on the South Course

The short par-4 14th on the South Course – one of the best tee shots on the property

'The Playground' is the world's largest putting green.

Before long, a heavy fog rolls in. Like, really heavy fog. I'm forced to slow down to eighty kilometres per hour, then sixty, then forty – I can only see about twenty metres ahead of me, the dense grey tube of the car headlights barely making an impact.

As I go further north, SH1 finally clears up and I close in on the gates of Te Arai Links. Being such a last-minute trip, I haven't arranged after-hours access to the resort. Instead, I fold down the back seats, get into my sleeping bag and settle in for a power nap before sunrise.

Waking from one of the worst sleeps of my life (who would have thought sleeping in the boot of the car wasn't a great solution?), I finally roll into Te Arai Links. The sight of the warm clubhouse and pristine fescue of the driving range is very welcome. Seeing my dishevelled state, the staff let me check in immediately and within fifteen minutes, I am showered, dressed and sitting in a golf cart with my camera gear, batteries fully charged. Well, camera batteries anyway – mentally, I'm just above empty, but nothing that an extremely strong coffee won't fix. As the glorious caffeine hits my lips, I look up for the first time and realise that conditions are nothing short of perfect. Some light clouds above the ocean look like they are on fire, and as the sun starts to peek over the horizon and reflects off the tranquil ocean, it's time to get to work.

I head straight for the 4th hole, a wild downhill par-4 framed by pines with a stunning coastal backdrop, and I know the trip has been worth it. The early morning rays filter through the pines onto the dew-covered fescue fairways, the deep green colour only revealed as ground staff make their mowing lines. The bold contours ripple and express themselves as I fly overhead, out towards the southern end of the uninhabited beach. Small but perfectly formed glassy waves are breaking quietly into the pristine fine white sands. Beyond, the Pacific Ocean appears to hold Great Barrier Island aloft, its distinctive silhouette providing a unique backdrop to the par-3 5th hole. The same pin flag that was being battered by wind and hail and bent sideways on my last visit is now completely still, the flag itself only offering an occasional gesture of a wave.

This is the Te Arai Links I had been hoping for ever since visiting the site during construction in 2018 and seeing this green site as pegged out by Coore & Crenshaw. Combining the natural beauty of this incredibly gifted site with the architecture, craft and finishing skills of Coore & Crenshaw and shapers Riley Johns and John Hawker is a recipe for truly outstanding golf. Add to that one of the best superintendents in the world in Brian Palmer keeping things firm and fast, and an accommodation and hospitality offer that covers every base, Te Arai Links almost asks you: what more do you want?

Later that morning, I'm lucky enough to play the South Course with Grace Rokela, Marketing Manager at Te Arai Links and former college golfer. We decide to have a match, but it is hardly fair. Not only am I trying to play vaguely decent golf on ninety minutes of sleep, Grace birdies all four par-3s, going 2-2-2-2 on the short holes. I don't think I've ever seen that before, and understandably she utterly destroys me in the match. Once we turn for home on the 15th, I feel drunk from the endlessly incredible scenery – the glassy waves haven't stopped breaking all day, and the golf course itself is a thing of beauty. The routing has variety, strategy and challenge in spades. As a course that will see many one-time golfers (as opposed to regular play from a members' course), there is a strong playability component. I didn't lose a ball all day, and the ground-game options, particularly around the greens, are plentiful. But if you want to shoot birdies, you will be forced to take on a riskier driving line or approach shot (or, like Grace, just stick it within twelve feet on every par-3!).

With fifteen holes boasting ocean views, each one distinctive and beautiful in their own way, picking favourite holes is near impossible. But as a (half) Australian, I have a soft spot for a short par-4, and the 14th is an excellent one, especially if the local surfers are catching few waves directly behind the green. I also loved the long right arc and elevated tee shot of the par-4 2nd, where the crack of the driver echoes back off the pines. But nothing compares to hitting a sweet drive off the 4th tee, way down to one of the steepest fairways I've ever seen – the Pacific Ocean backdrop a nice bonus. Actually, hitting the 'high-road' line on the 6th was just as good. As was hitting across the dunes on 8. Fifteen through 18 is also a superb finish. I could go on, but would eventually name every hole.

Simplicity and restraint at its finest on the par-3 5th on the South Course

Te Arai Links is a truly world-class golf destination, and worthy of a visit from any serious golfer who is interested in playing the very best the game has to offer. And that's just the South Course.

The next morning, I tour the soon to open North Course with the managing partner, Jim Rohrstafff, whose passion for golf is palpable with every purposeful stride he makes onto the virgin turf of Tom Doak's latest work. By the end of the walk-and-talk, I'm convinced the whole 'no-gutter thing' is probably due to Jim's incredible eye for detail and drive for perfection. His knowledge and deep sense for every inch of a course that hasn't even been played yet is quite amazing.

After the North Course tour, I bump into Australian comedian and golfer Mick Malloy, who's keen for a rundown of what I've seen out on the North Course. After giving my impressions of the wild, expansive terrain and routing, he concludes, 'So he's gone full Doak then?' It's probably a good summary, although it will take another visit to find out for sure. I love a good excuse to get back to Te Arai Links.

LEFT Te Arai Links South Course with the 11th green in the foreground

Above the 4th, 5th and 6th of the North Course

Attempt Three – Northern Lights

Third time lucky, I think as I drive through the gates and into the moody pine forest that separates Te Arai Links from the rolling hinterland. It's a phrase usually reserved for when things have gone badly the first two times, and one is hoping for some respite from the gods before throwing in the towel. But even though my first trip was a washout, it still had some amazing moments. My second trip, just over twelve months earlier, brought one of the best golf experiences of my life, getting 'drunk' on the scenery of the South Course and northern New Zealand's incredible coastline. So in this instance, 'third time lucky' really just means I've been lucky enough to come here three times. Actually, more, if you include the visit while construction on the South Course was still under way, when myself and my wife got bogged in the sand dunes with Riley Johns, who was out here shaping greens for Coore & Crenshaw, and a couple of visits to the incredible Tara Iti, just up the road.

But this trip is just as exciting, with Tom Doak's new North Course now open and ready for play. While there are still construction projects and finishing touches happening around the property, the golf is, for now at least, complete. Fine emerald fescue, bright white sand and sparkling blue ocean. It's the sort of minimalist aesthetic that calms the mind and allows the golf to shine while also being jaw-droppingly beautiful at every turn.

Contours connect the 7th and 4th greens on the North Course

After a relatively smooth trip across 'the ditch' from Melbourne, I arrive mid-afternoon, check in and secure a golf cart for the sunset session. Being based at the South Course, it makes sense to take a cruise through some of the more familiar holes of the Coore & Crenshaw gem, to see how they've evolved over the last year or so, before making my way across to the North. Unsurprisingly, the South is looking superb, melting into the landscape with even more ease as the vegetation matures. After an obligatory photo from the 14th tee, one of my favourite holes on the property, I stop on the 15th tee of the South Course and look over to the 17th green of the North Course, with a view down the rollicking par-5 18th beyond.

What Doak might have created if afforded a larger slice of the coastal land is a tantalising prospect. Standing here, looking at Doak's audacious 18th, I imagine even Bill Coore must smile and shake his head at its boldness. Turning back to Coore's 15th on the South Course, I'm struck by how often these two masters work in close proximity. The last time I saw their courses intertwined like this was at Streamsong Resort, where Doak's Blue and Coore's Red courses dance together. Barnbougle and Lost Farm offer another point of comparison, though separated by a river. The contrast in styles here is just as striking – Coore's calm, considered and stunningly beautiful 15th invites you to play, while Doak's 18th *dares* you to do the same.

Of the course boundaries and how they were decided, managing director Jim Rohrstaff describes how it all played out: 'When Bill first came out, we just said, "Have a look around, here's the whole property." We drove around for a couple of days and let him walk for a while. When he asked about the boundaries for the two courses, we told him to pretend like there was just one course there and we'd figure out the rest. Bill really took that to heart – I think if he could have somehow figured out how to get a clubhouse that stretched from the 1st to the 18th and just taken up eighteen holes along the edge of the water, he would have. He's a country gentleman, but he's got some real teeth to him! He was quite happy to take all of the prime land, knowing there was another course going in, and really focused on the coastline.

'It's interesting – in our documentary you see Bill and Tom cross paths on site, actually trading keys because Tom was getting Bill's vehicle. It was the first time they'd seen each other in almost five years. Bill gave Tom a bit of grief, saying, "Well, I gave you some land back" because he had actually extended a little less than originally planned. But Tom, to his credit, was given the northern portion of the coastline, and as he and Brian Slawnik started to explore, they were just giddy with excitement saying, "Bill didn't even look here – this is the most unbelievable, interesting golf land."'

The par-5 18th tee view on Te Arai Links South Course

> 'Te Arai Links is a truly world-class golf destination, and worthy of a visit from any serious golfer who is interested in playing the very best the game has to offer.'

The land they found, over a massive dune ridge and deep in the plantation pine forest, is quite extraordinary. The scale, elevation and bold contouring is at first intimidating, and then endlessly intriguing. Without the distraction of the ocean, the Renaissance Golf team was able to focus intently on the ground in front of them, and uncovered a different type of interest and drama. Given the shaping talent involved on the project, it's impossible to discern how much of the contouring was 'in the ground' versus touched by the blade of the 'dozer. But it is a fair bet that not much was softened in the construction process.

The resulting greens are, for the imaginative golfer, utterly irresistible. Often I found myself wishing my approach to land out of position just so I could use some of the surrounding contours to bring myself back into play. Sometimes, I didn't even have to bother with the approach shot at all – anything within fifty metres was quite puttable, given the firm, tight fescue approach zones, which blend seamlessly into the putting surfaces. Watching the ball roll, bend and accelerate over such surfaces never gets old – you're playing with gravity and physics in the most fun way imaginable. While the 4th and 7th greens form an incredible visual feast of undulations, the short par-4 6th features the most extreme example of these contours. Dubbed the 'taco green' for its distinctive shape, the flag barely peeks out from behind the natural shapes of the sand, rising well above head height in some parts.

The rollicking visuals of the 18th on the North Course

The dramatic uphill par-5 11th of the North Course

It's not fair to characterise the North Course as a purely inland adventure – six holes play with a spectacular ocean backdrop (1, 2, 8, 16, 17 and 18) and two more have ocean views behind the tee (3 and 9). But in comparison with South's remarkable fifteen oceanfront holes, it certainly has a greater variety of settings. That the routing returns to the ocean for the 8th and 9th breaks up the round nicely. The par-5 9th should be an awkward hole given it demands an uphill drive, blind second shot and has a road running right through it, but it plays amazingly well, a feat of great design and quality construction.

Two holes later, another par-5, the 11th, is equally intimidating. This time you can see the flag clearly from the tee, it's just that it looks so far away, and is perched on top of a huge sand dune. To the right of the green is a massive drop to a natural sand blowout, which also forms part of a hazardous approach for the brilliant par-4 13th. The 14th is another grand par-5, this time with sandy waste all up the left, and plenty of angles need to be negotiated to hold onto another boldly shaped green. After the shapely par-3 15th, the 16th is one of the coolest tee shots on the course, from high up on the same ridge that the 9th traverses. Much like the 1st hole, the bowl-shaped green is drivable if the wind is favourable, but brings risk if you miss the target. All throughout the round, if you hit out of position, you will be sternly challenged.

Mirroring the South Course, the routing finishes with a par-3 17th with a skyline green and crashing waves beyond, and a dramatic par-5 18th, which runs along the coast. Sitting with a cold beverage, overlooking the 18th green at the Cheshire Architects-designed North Course clubhouse, and watching surfers drink in the last rays of sun on Te Arai Point, this time it's me shaking my head. *They've done it again.*

Over the course of my stay, I caught up with managing partners Ric Kayne and Jim Rohrstaff. I'm keen to learn some of the philosophy behind Te Arai Links, and why it is such a successful execution. Kayne's vision is refreshingly simple. 'We want to make this fun,' he explains. 'We want people to walk off the 18th hole saying, "I haven't had quite enough, I want to go again."'

Rohrstaff adds, 'While many courses were being stretched to egregious lengths, we took a different approach. These courses have plenty of challenge, but they're fundamentally fun.'

This philosophy extends to how they approached the entire project. 'We're more producers than directors,' Kayne says. 'We chose what we thought were Picasso and Monet, and we didn't tell them how to paint. We just said, "Here's your canvas, go nuts, do your best." We knew we were giving them extraordinary property to work with.' He adds with a smile, 'Though we did remind them that another great painter would be working here too, so they might want to do their best job.'

The result is a place that transcends golf. 'Even those who don't play know it's a special place to be,' says Kayne. 'We want people to have fun, but to respect that it's a shared experience. We've curated our membership and the people involved so they know how to have fun while being mindful of others.'

If there's a better golf destination in the world, I'm not aware of it. The combination of natural beauty, exceptional golf and hospitality, and a truly welcoming atmosphere is simply unmatched.

Top down over the North Course's inland loop

BRIAN PALMER

WORDS & PHOTOGRAPHY
BY WILLIAM WATT

'We live in a great outdoor area. It's all about the outdoors and I don't know, there just aren't many times where I'm like, "Hey, I want to go watch TV".'

BRIAN PALMER

I first met Brian Palmer in 2017, shortly after playing at Shoreacres, a beautiful Seth Raynor course outside Chicago. But it was a few hours earlier, on the driveway into the course and before I knew his name, that I first became enamoured with his work. I had done a double-take as the morning sun hit the fairway of the first hole – it looked like a giant putting green.

After I rolled a birdie putt straight into a bunker on the back nine, with Brian watching on and quietly chuckling at my fate, I knew this was a man to watch.

Cutting Pins at Tara Iti

Brian Palmer is someone who lives and breathes golf. As the son of a superintendent who followed his father's path into the world of golf, he's been walking the fairways his whole life. During a recent visit, we spent a typically stunning Kiwi sunrise cutting some fresh hole locations at Tara Iti, the place Brian has been charged with keeping firm and fast (and occasionally a bit fiery). With his appointment to Director of Courses across both Tara Iti and Te Arai Links, we caught up about the demands of maintaining three very different golf courses and some of the trends he's seeing in the industry (as well as getting a little sidetracked by the price of pineapples).

Do you still get out and do this [cut pins] occasionally?

Brian Palmer: We change a couple holes a day here and there, and one of my other guys has slowly become a core set-up man – he's got a good eye. So probably not as much as when I first started, and I definitely do it more in the summer! We've got a wide variety of projects going on, it's kind of wild. I never thought I'd be looking after some of this stuff when I came here. I thought it was just a golf course. It's so much more. Keeps me on my toes, that's for sure.

What are some of the trends you are interested in at the moment in the turf industry?

BP: I'm pretty old-school and can be a bit of a curmudgeon, but autonomous mowers are certainly getting closer. It'll be weird because it'll put some guys out of a job, but that's a ways down the track yet. We just got another GPS sprayer in. That's pretty damn cool, seeing just how quickly we can spray the surfaces and not have to drop any foam as they're so accurate.

Is that a ground sprayer or a drone?

BP: Ground. But there are drone sprayers. I know of some larger resorts in the States that'll do steep bunker banks and stuff like that with the drone, and again, the accuracy and the precision is just amazing. Currently, there's a chance for human error in a lot of these applications, so that's exciting for me looking forward to seeing how technology can improve our processes and accuracy.

But overall, as an industry, we really haven't evolved that much. There's a lawnmower museum in Southport, England, where they've got some of the very first greens mowers, they must be about 120 years old. And it's really not any different than what we have today. Yes, we've got some bells and whistles these days, but it's got a reel, it's got a bed knife, it's a gravity-fed gas tank with a fan on the engine to cool it off. Old-school stuff certainly works in greenkeeping, but it's about time that we start progressing and trying to keep up with everything else. In agriculture, GPS autonomous vehicles have been around forever. But here, we've never had it. I think it's because we're such a small sector. Even though we think we're big, because this is what we live and breathe, in reality, golf and golf technology is such a small part of the industry.

I noticed back in the office you had some large screens with pretty detailed maps and blinking lights and so on ...

BP: Yeah, the irrigation systems have come a long way. We have just upgraded to some new software so that we can actually see if a sprinkler head is going to fail. It's smart enough to say, 'Hey, there's a drop or a spike in power. Keep an eye on that sprinkler head.' Whereas before, you didn't know it was bad until it was dead, and that's too late. Thinking more about water usage. I can actually water the course off my phone and adjust programs on the fly. I could be out walking like we are today and say, 'You know what? I don't like this hump. This is too dry, or too wet,' and adjust the program so that when it runs this evening, it'll be fixed by morning. So precision watering has changed quite a bit, which is important because golf courses are under the microscope. I mean, we're not producing any food or anything. It's just a game, you know? And we're using up a lot of the world's precious resources to grow grass for a game. There's a lot of people who don't think we should be using it at all. In Melbourne, you guys are doing anything you can to catch and collect water for your golf courses on The Sandbelt. And here, it's no different. We collect our groundwater from our pumps – soon we're going to be updating our pumps to be able to reverse the flow and ship water up to our main reservoir. It's pretty wild.

So there's not much in the way of electrification of general equipment?

BP: There is a little bit. They've got two electric vehicles at [Te Arai] Links. Electric carts have been around forever, but as you know, how clean are those batteries? What are we doing to the environment to mine resources for the batteries, and how do we dispose of them? There certainly is that debate.

Some of the chemistries we use have changed as well. Not that long ago, you would be spraying lead and mercury and all sorts of different stuff on courses. If it's to keep Poa out or if it's to spray for diseases, your main fungicide for a long time was just straight mercury. We're so environmentally conscious now with what we spray and how we spray, and the thresholds that we can use.

We look after these places in such a different manner than any of my predecessors. I remember getting to Shoreacres [the esteemed private golf club just outside Chicago] and going through the shed and there was a pile in the corner with a tarp over it, with these huge wheelbarrows holding the tarp down.

I ask the long-time assistant, 'Yo, Ralph. What's underneath those tarps?'

And he's like, 'Oh, jefe, that is some *bad shit*.'

I was like, 'Well, what is it, Ralph?'

'I don't know,' he says.

I take off the tarp and it says, *Lead Arsenate*. We're not spraying anything like that these days. Everything now is very targeted in the way our irrigation systems are designed. We can go watering products to the right depth pretty easily nowadays. Luckily working with fescue in a humid climate like we have here, we don't spray a whole lot of fungicides. Maybe an application or two a year.

Moving from the United States to a remote part of New Zealand was obviously a big move for you personally. What has that experience been like?

BP: It's funny, people I meet out on the course or around town are often like, 'Oh, what'd you come over here for?' as if I was just passing through and happened to take up this role at one of the best golf courses in the world. And I say, 'Well, I'm here for the job.' For people that aren't in the golf world, they often don't realise this is a profession, and a super competitive one too. They also often don't appreciate the scale of the job and what goes into it. I mean, I manage a pretty big team, and a fair amount of money. I also need to be across the fine details of chemistries, irrigation, then tackle the challenges of staffing in a remote location and ensuring the training is all up to standard.

Can you run us through your daily routine?

BP: I like to wake up pretty early, I've always been an early riser. I'm up at 4 am and try to do some sort of workout at home, then be in here in my office at 5 am. I really like a bit of time in the morning to get everything set. Most of the crew start at 6 am, but I like myself, assistants and mechanic to come in and help make sure mowers are all parked outside, set up, ready to rock and roll so that when that morning meeting is done, it's like, 'OK guys, hop on your mower and go!'

That routine allows me to get a game plan together, get some emails done and then hopefully, be able to cut cups like today, or even just go for a walk out on the course. Sometimes it's nice to just walk this place and traipse over some dunes. It might not appear as if I'm doing a whole hell of a lot, but I'm always learning more about the property and what we have to do and need to stay on top of.

In the summer, we're always watching moisture. So if it's a hot summer's day, there's definitely some extra watering involved. I love hand watering, so I'll be out on a hose in the mornings and do a preliminary irrigation set-up after walking the course and seeing the course set up.

Getting it all dialled in makes the end of the day easier when I can be like, 'Actually, you know what, everything we set up is looking good.' Before leaving someone will make a quick loop on the course to make sure everything is right.

The end of my workday varies between 3 to 6 pm, depending on what has been happening that day. Then I go home and try to get down to the beach for a swim. I love to cook, so then I'll go and make a nice dinner, have a good cocktail or beer, and that's about it. Pretty simple.

You mentioned last time we caught up that you were growing fruit?

BP: Yeah, we've got a bit of this and that. The bananas have taken off crazy so we've got quite a few bunches of bananas that are in the process of ripening right now. The mandarins are going crazy, so we've got a tree covered in them. And we've got oranges and peaches not far behind. Not only do I like grass, but I like all plants; it's fun. It's just a wild climate here as well – subtropical, really. So there really isn't a frost so I can grow pretty much whatever I want. There's a guy with a pineapple plantation up in the Whangārei Heads up there. You can see it from here. He's got like 20,000 plants.

Did you know pineapples used to cost like $20,000 each?

BP: Really?

Yeah, way back in the 1700s, they were super rare in Europe as they were almost impossible to grow. They became a symbol of wealth and power, a luxury item of its day, and people would just carry them around under their arm. You could even rent a pineapple just to show off to your friends at a dinner party. Then, as steamships came to prominence, they became more attainable and eventually lost their luxurious lustre completely.

BP: I was just in Hawaii for the first time and had some of the best fresh pineapples I've ever eaten. They're just everywhere over there, and they're so good.

Yeah, it's an underrated fruit these days.

BP: Totally is.

What are you watching at the moment?

BP: I don't have a TV.

Was not having a TV a conscious choice to not get sucked into the news cycle?

BP: I don't know, I just don't watch much and my wife doesn't really at all. She's a voracious reader. She rifles through books *at pace*. She's the only person I've ever seen brushing her teeth and reading a book, or just walking around the house with it. But yeah, we live in a great outdoor area. It's all about the outdoors and I don't know, there just aren't many times where I'm like, 'Hey, I want to go watch TV.' Every now and again, we will, I'll watch a couple shows on Netflix or YouTube on the laptop about cooking or something like that. But that's about it.

What about music?

BP: I'm a big music lover. I'm all over the place too. I love bluegrass, some old school country, love a fair amount of hip hop, and a bunch of indie rock. I was just listening to the Shins the other day, and there's a bluegrass band I really love called Trampled by Turtles. I listen to them quite a bit. I like some of the rock down here, what do they call it? Psych, surf rock – like the Daily J. There's another local band here called Sojourn that's quite good. They're from Mangawhai actually – James, one of our caddies, is their guitarist. Also there's a new album from the lead singer of The Roots, Black Thought and Danger Mouse – it is pretty killer.

I like albums too – no playlists. I go all the way through an album and that's how I know if it's a good artist or not. It's one thing to like a song, but I want to be able to listen to the album.

I was chatting with Mike Cocking about music and he was saying that designing a golf course is a lot like making an album.

BP: Yeah. It's got to have a certain rhythm to it.

Over eighteen holes, you don't want it to all be at full volume. If Tara Iti is an album, what's the best part of the album for you?

BP: Yeah, this is something we talk about a lot. Fifteen to 18 are really good. I mean, if there's a single pinnacle, a couple phenomenal golf holes, it's probably 8 and 9, and they're almost sleepers in a way because they're not oceanfront or ocean views. And people don't really speak about them or photograph them. But for me it's 8 and 9 – I could hit the rewind button and play them over and over. Whenever I play a little loop out here, four to six holes or whatever, it usually includes 8, 9 and 4, at least one of that bunch.

With thirty-six holes at Te Arai Links recently coming under your direction, what are some of the new challenges and opportunities that this larger role presents for you?

BP: I like a challenge and this certainly presents me with one! It is a great opportunity for the superintendents of all three courses to grow. In the future, it will be a great opportunity to promote from within and try to develop a homegrown team of greenkeepers.

With each course at a different stage in its development cycle, how useful is it to have seen Tara Iti evolve, and know to some extent what's coming at you this time around?

BP: The courses are so different in their architectural styles and their locations that the environment has a different effect on all three. Tara Iti has evolved quickly because it is very exposed and the bunker style has steep faces that allows sand to move around. There are vast sand expanses in between holes that are meant to be kept clean of vegetation so that sand can really move around. Te Arai Links South does not have as much exposed sand as Tara Iti and so it will not move around as much, other than a few holes. Te Arai Links North is very young, and very different from the others. The bunkers have grass faces so that will help keep sand in them. Several holes are in the woods, which will keep the wind from blowing through as much as the other two courses. As for working with fescue surfaces, we have learned that as it matures it really starts to take care of itself. I have learned a lot about the species and plan to implement a lot of what we do at Tara Iti at Te Arai Links.

BANDON DUNES: FIELD OF DREAMS

OREGON, USA

WORDS BY SHAUN TOLSON
PHOTOGRAPHY BY BRIAN MCSHALLEY
AND MATT CARDIS

Twenty-five years after Bandon Dunes unveiled its first rendition of American links along the rugged, windswept shores of southern Oregon, the celebrated resort remains dedicated to its mission to deliver 'golf as it was meant to be'.

If Hollywood was ever granted the rights to tell the story of Bandon Dunes, the resulting movie would likely open with developer Mike Keiser walking among the many gorse bushes that once covered the heavily contoured parcel of land upon which the resort is set. Soon, a voice would echo out, 'If you build it, they will come.'

Keiser, then almost fifty years old, might scan the rugged hillsides searching for the source of the message. In its place, the vision of a series of fairways – their terrain rumpled and pockmarked with occasional pot bunkers and strewn with tufts of wiry, maritime grasses – would be laid out in front of him. He'd see these golfing corridors angling towards and playing alongside dramatic cliffs that plummeted away to the Pacific Ocean surging below. And, in that moment, he would conceive the idea for a sprawling golf resort that transported authentic links golf from the British Isles, replanting it in southern Oregon soil.

That would be the cinematic birth of one of America's most celebrated modern golf resorts. And it would be almost entirely fictitious. Almost.

It's been more than twenty-five years since Keiser's first effort to create an authentic and compelling landscape for public golf was introduced to the world. In the late 1990s, he and a young, brash – but notably skilled – Scottish course designer carved eighteen holes across a windswept, gorse-covered landscape that spilled away to the Pacific. Together, they created an American resort that delivers an unbridled golf experience as rooted in the history of the game as Britain's heralded links, and embraces the aesthetic of those celebrated courses.

There's no shortage of things that can happen in a quarter of a century, and plenty can change – and has – at Bandon Dunes. Yet, for all the ways the resort has evolved, growing bigger, more sophisticated and more refined, it's never wavered from a foundational ideology: to deliver 'golf as it was meant to be'. Such a reality is the by-product of two key factors: the man who founded the resort, and the land upon which that golfing utopia was and continues to be built.

Early Beginnings

Keiser had played many of the best courses in the United States, most of which were the strictly guarded property of highly exclusive private clubs. It was Keiser's first belief that every golfer should have access to similar, high-quality experiences. But, years earlier, the now eighty-year-old had also fallen in love with some of Britain's and Ireland's most remote courses, destinations such as Royal Dornoch and Ballybunion. The sprawling site in Oregon that Keiser discovered during the early 1990s – hundreds of acres blanketed by gorse, shore pines, cedar-and-spruce forests and dunes covered with sea grasses – boasted all of the innate character that made those Scottish and Irish courses so impactful. Despite that discovery, there was a moment when Bandon Dunes almost became the golf resort that was never built.

Keiser is cut from a unique cloth. He sets his priorities on a single attribute: the golf course. 'Golf first,' he says. But then he's quick to add, 'Golf is enough.' In that respect, it's not difficult to understand how every course with Keiser's backing has matured into a celebrated venue. With no desire to balance fairways with residential real estate, Keiser is focused exclusively on finding the best parcels of land for each hole. In that way, Keiser – as a commissioning boss – is every golf course architect's dream employer.

Yet, because he's passionate about the game, because he's well-travelled and has seen many of the world's most celebrated courses and because he knows what has made lasting impressions on him as a golfer (and what hasn't), Keiser is opinionated. Moreover, because he's the one investing millions of dollars, he makes a point to evaluate each hole before it's built.

During preliminary phases of a course's conception, after a proposed routing is determined but before any sizeable work has been done to move or clear the ground, Keiser walks the layout, scoring each of the holes on a scale of one to ten. He judges them almost exclusively on the visceral response that golfers are likely to have while playing. 'On every hole, I imagine that you and I are teeing off and what we're thinking,' he says. 'When we get the "holy shit" moments, the score I give that hole is at least a seven. And when [the first impression] is "really holy shit!", the score would be an eight or nine. I don't go much higher than that.'

Such a system can rub some architects the wrong way. Tom Doak, who's worked with Keiser on multiple projects – including two courses at Bandon Dunes – is nothing if not candid on the topic. 'Honestly, I don't like his "scoring" of holes one bit,' he says, adding that while Keiser's methodology is similar to his own, it's likely that the developer can sometimes have difficulty envisioning the final product if the site is unkempt and requires significant vegetation removal. 'Maybe Mike giving some hole a five out of ten and calling it "an architect's hole" is motivating to me to make it really shine,' he adds. 'I think Mike thinks so, anyway.'

With this system in place, Keiser walked the initial routing of the resort's eponymous course with its architect, David McLay Kidd. Upon completion of the tour, Keiser matter-of-factly told the course designer he was four holes short. 'You've got an eighteen-hole routing, but four of the holes are real dogs and I'm not going any further.'

According to Keiser, McLay Kidd petitioned to still move forward with the project, to trust him that the course would be better than Keiser perceived. Keiser wouldn't budge. In retrospect, Keiser acknowledges, 'David probably would've worn me down [by saying] that fourteen good holes is better than zero.' Such a battle of attrition wasn't necessary. Shortly after he told McLay Kidd that his routing was incomplete, Keiser learned that 400 acres of neighbouring land was up for sale because the landowner was forced to declare bankruptcy. In the next breath, McLay Kidd not only had a swath of new land upon which to build four stunning holes, but Keiser had enough land to build a second course – so long as his initial venture proved successful.

Winning Formula

Early on in Bandon Dunes' existence, Keiser adhered to a formula that defies the laws of mathematics. He asserted that 1 + 1 = 3. In Keiser's estimation, a resort with two courses was more than just the sum of its parts, and as Pacific Dunes opened along Oregon's southern coast in 2001, the resort's second course in many ways legitimised the fledgling property. 'One course is a curiosity,' Keiser has often said. 'Two courses is a destination.'

Designed by Tom Doak, Pacific Dunes did more than just impact the public's perception of the resort; it challenged preconceived notions about how a course should be laid out. In simple terms, Pacific Dunes proved that a design that surrenders itself to the topography of a site can produce captivating and stunning golfing experiences – even when the course's back nine includes three par-5s, only two par-4s and begins with back-to-back par-3s. 'I think many outsiders felt that it was very bold,' Keiser says of the decision to build a course with such an unconventional scorecard. 'But Tom and I both felt that the routing fit the site perfectly. Today, more architects let the land determine the golf course, but it certainly wasn't prevalent back then.'

Looking back on his experience working with Keiser on Pacific Dunes – and then again, when he was involved in the creation of the resort's fourth course, Old Macdonald, almost a decade later – Doak commends the developer for never getting ahead of himself, even at a point when there was enough evidence to suggest that he seemingly could do no wrong. 'The sole mission was to design and build the best course that we could,' Doak says. 'There were no concessions to making it fit well with the next course, such as changing the sequence so the pro shop could be reused.'

As the course architect acknowledges, Keiser's rationale was that if they didn't create the very best course that they could, they might not get the opportunity to create another one. 'I think it's a huge reason that each and every course has been such a success.'

Not to be discounted, Keiser's approach to working with each architect and the ways in which he removes himself from the process (at least after his preliminary rating of each prospective hole) are additional drivers that ultimately set Bandon Dunes up for success. 'Every time I was on site, Mike was too, but mostly he'd go play golf while we worked, and then walk around with me once or twice to check on the progress and ask questions,' Doak recalls. 'He would rarely say he didn't like something. Instead, he would ask why we were building a particular bunker. I think Mike is the only client I've ever had who suggested taking a bunker out, as opposed to adding one.'

In Bill Coore's estimation, when it comes to developers, Keiser sits in a tier all of his own. 'He's the most wonderful example of how to encourage people to be creative, how to give them sites that are amazing and naturally gifted for golf, and how to give them the freedom to work with those sites.'

Landforms

During the resort's twenty-fifth anniversary celebration in May 2024, a fireside chat with many of the course architects who have worked on projects at Bandon Dunes revealed stories of discovery. More specifically, during the routing of several layouts, parcels of land were cleared accidentally, which introduced new playing corridors that ultimately replaced previously planned sequences of holes. Such a unique attribute is an even greater testament to the quality of the land upon which Bandon Dunes is built, and the seemingly endless possibilities that exist there.

The same can be said for the diversity of the land itself, especially on neighbouring plots, which allows courses like Bandon Dunes, Pacific Dunes and Old Macdonald to stand out with such distinction, even as they figuratively rub elbows and steal glances at one another. 'While building Pacific Dunes, I remember standing on the 14th tee and looking over at the site that I knew someday could be another golf course and thinking, "Wow, somebody is going to get a chance to build something there,"' says course architect Jim Urbina. 'Little did I know it was going to be me, and the course would be Old Macdonald.'

In fact, those three layouts all resemble classic Scottish and Irish links courses in different ways, which means golfers might initially conclude that one is a more authentic interpretation than the others. It's only upon further reflection that they'll realise that each is equally successful for bringing across the pond classic links courses of different scale. Those characteristics were also top of mind for the architects during the construction process.

'You had to be careful as you walked around Pacific Dunes, because the features were much smaller,' says Urbina. 'Pacific Dunes was built on the ground, meaning the subtleties of the dunes were hard to decipher. I was afraid to touch everything at Pacific Dunes, if that makes sense. I was afraid to over-do a green, to over-shape those features, to add too many bunkers – to make the experience at Pacific Dunes too big, because it was a more intimate site.

'But with Old Macdonald,' he continues, 'Mike Keiser challenged us to go to the other side of that golf design architecture – to get bigger, to get bolder, to do the things that we would have never considered at Pacific Dunes. The landforms were going to be bigger because the site was bigger and the dunes were bigger. Pacific Dunes was on the ground and intimate, and with Old Macdonald, I knew it would be the opposite.'

In many respects, Bandon Trails, the third course at Bandon Dunes, was as much a contrast to the first two courses that preceded it. Trails doesn't play alongside dramatic cliffs that tumble down to the ocean. Instead, it ventures deep into the temperate rainforest. When Bill Coore and Ben Crenshaw took on the project, they understood its inherent challenges. 'When we set out to work at Bandon Trails,' Coore explains, 'the goal was to build a course that somehow would be able to measure up, at least to the point of being considered a complement to golf at Bandon Dunes, but also to be a complement to that site and reflect what that site is about.'

Some who have visited the resort and played each of the courses will never rank Bandon Trails above the others for the simple fact that the course doesn't offer the same dramatic oceanfront vistas. Others will conclude that Bandon Trails' routing through the conifer trees makes it authentically rooted in the Pacific Northwest, and thereby they might prefer it over the more exposed courses along the coast. One thing is unequivocally true: resort guests' rankings of each of the courses is likely to change each time they visit.

Coore & Crenshaw weren't denied the opportunity to work along those aforementioned cliffs either. In 2020, Sheep Ranch, the latest full-length course at Bandon Dunes, opened on the northernmost stretch of the property. It immediately displayed the duo's routing prowess while also incorporating a quirky feature. By the time golfers reach the halfway mark of their rounds there, they will have stood on six greens perched right on the edge of the bluff overlooking the Pacific Ocean. In total, the course features nine holes that either hug the edge of that bluff from tee to green or culminate with ocean-side putting surfaces. 'The routing that Bill and Ben did is proof of their genius,' says Keiser.

For all the dramatic and unobstructed views of the ocean that Sheep Ranch delivers, one thing that golfers won't see while on the course is sand – at least not in the form of on-course bunkers. The course's location is the most exposed of any area of the resort, which means the land is constantly battered by gusty winds. It was deemed that those winds would make it difficult to keep the necessary amounts of sand in the bunkers. Additionally, those winds alone provide a stout defence against low scores. 'Had we given Bill and Ben the greenlight to include sand bunkers, they'd probably have ten,' Keiser acknowledges. 'In part because of the exposure to the wind but also because it's such a natural site that it didn't need it.'

In keeping with the tradition of building courses that naturally fit the land, the newest addition to Bandon's lineup, Shorty's, is a nineteen-hole short course set just south of Bandon Preserve and just west of Bandon Trails. The layout tumbles over and around a swath of dramatically shaped dunes and ridges – dunes that Keith Cutten, who co-designed the course with his colleagues at WAC Golf, describes as 'the biggest' and 'most choppy' on the entire property. The plot of land is one that had been earmarked as a potential golf course site for years, but Keiser and his team recognised that any full-length layout would require total manipulation of the land.

Such an action would be out of character for how Bandon Dunes approaches its courses, and so, the team waited until the timing and project were right. Their patience was finally rewarded with a masterpiece of golf in miniature form – an answer to the hypothetical musing of what golf might look like in the land of hobbits. 'On some of our shorter holes, you get this sense of compression as you come into certain areas because the dunes squeeze you,' Cutten says. 'And we play off of that on the next hole, which opens up into a huge bowl. You really feel the contrast and scale of these dunes.'

A Good Walk

When Keiser set out to build Bandon Dunes, he wasn't content to merely build links courses in a remote area. Replicating the look and feel of iconic layouts such as Ballybunion and Royal Dornoch was only part of the objective. The other element was replicating the experience that comes with playing those esteemed British courses – and that couldn't be done with a fleet of golf carts.

In his biggest gamble, Keiser pushed in all of his chips on one pivotal detail: that the original golf course (and all subsequent layouts) would be walking only. 'Our byline is "golf as it was meant to be", which some people think is a bit arrogant,' he says, 'but it's a walking sport, so we have caddies. And eight-five per cent of the rounds that are played at Bandon Dunes are played with caddies.'

It might be presumptuous to say that such a commitment served as a major selling point to McLay Kidd, who grew up playing courses in southern Scotland with a bag slung over his shoulders. After all, the young course designer was just setting out to develop his own brand when the opportunity to work with Keiser came along. It is safe to say, however, that the developer immediately found a comrade-in-arms.

'In every avenue of life, we're all striving for authenticity and experience,' McLay Kidd says. 'But when you play golf in a beautiful place without walking, you're getting neither. You don't get to take in the fresh air or see the view or chuckle with your buddies as you walk the fairways.

'If you're going to a place like Bandon in order to experience the landscape, the environment, the weather, how do you do it from a golf cart?' he asks. 'You can't. Walking is the purest form of playing golf. You're feeling the wind and the temperature and the softness of the surface. Just those things alone make a huge difference in a golf shot.'

Could Bandon Dunes have succeeded had Keiser acquiesced to the predominant playing style of American golfers, that being one spent behind the wheel of a golf cart for much of the day? Not in McLay Kidd's estimation. 'Bandon Dunes with golf carts would have withered on the vine within the first few years,' he says. 'It would've failed ... I am positive of that.'

Reflection Point

It would be easy now for Keiser to look back on his long exploratory walks searching for the right parcel of land to build a remote resort that could deliver a golf experience stripped of the excesses that had come to define the American version of the pastime and say it was all by design. It would be simple and painless for him to say that he had fostered a grand vision for what Bandon Dunes would someday become. After all, Keiser was a founding member of Sand Hills Golf Club in rural Nebraska, a private club that – when it opened in the mid-1990s – immediately proved that exceptional golf and remote destinations can coexist in the United States. That said, it was one thing for Sand Hills to establish such a model in the private club sector; it was quite another for Keiser to attempt to prove the success of that same model with a public resort.

Rather than make bold assertions that he always had a plan for Bandon Dunes, Keiser instead is guileless. 'My prayer was to break even,' he says. 'Everyone I knew, plus me, thought it was a crazy idea. A links golf course in Bandon, Oregon ... it made no sense.'

As McLay Kidd's layout neared its completion during the first quarter of 1999, everyone involved in the project took a stab at predicting the total number of rounds that would be played in its first year. To break even, the resort needed to book 10,000 rounds. Some involved in the project didn't think the resort would be that lucky. Once the season began and reservations came in, however, Keiser and company saw that they would greatly exceed even their most cautiously optimistic expectations. By the end of that first year, almost 25,000 rounds of golf had been played at the resort.

'We've all learned that remoteness is not the bad thing that we all thought it was,' Keiser says. 'The remoteness of Bandon Dunes makes it, now in hindsight, part of the winning formula. It's the appeal. And it's somewhat startling to say that this place in the middle of nowhere – that you have to work hard to get to – is as attractive as it is.'

'Bandon Dunes with golf carts would have withered on the vine within the first few years,' McLay Kidd says. 'It would've failed ... I am positive of that.'

The success of Bandon Dunes can't be overstated, and it's impossible to ignore. The first time that Tom Doak's wife joined him on a trip to the resort, she immediately remarked that she had never seen so many happy men in one place.

Bill Coore perceives the resort's success slightly differently. 'You can hear people at Bandon having discussions about the best and worst courses at the resort,' he explains. 'Nowhere else in the world that I know of, can you go to a place with two, three, four or more golf courses and hear that kind of discussion. It just doesn't happen. But at Bandon, you can sit there and listen to people talk about five golf courses, and each one has its own following, particularly amongst people who've played out there more than once. I just know of no other place in the world like it.' To that end, Coore doesn't hesitate to proclaim Keiser 'the most influential developer of golf courses in the world in the past quarter century'.

When asked directly about his own legacy, Keiser's answer isn't nearly as reverent. 'It's simple,' he says. 'That I've helped to redefine what golf in America can be, both in terms of links style and in terms of great golf that is available to the public.

'It's quite amazing that Bandon Dunes is a hit,' he adds with candour. 'Who knew?'

The voice that called out among the gorse bushes might be the answer to his question, but that's only if Hollywood is telling the story.

BANDON BY THE SEA OREGON, USA

WORDS AND PHOTOGRAPHY BY AKBAR CHISTI

The guest services job offer came out of nowhere. I'd just finished playing Pacific Dunes at Bandon for the first time in late 2001 – mind still reeling from the experience – when head golf professional Jim Wakeman emerged from the back of the shop and said, 'You know, if you want a job, we can have you here working next week.'

I was nineteen years old, and that casual offer would change the course of my life.

But let me back up. My first encounter with Bandon Dunes came two years earlier.

1999

In October 1999, at age sixteen, my mother, father and little brother, Ali, and I went to Bandon Dunes to play it for the first time. The only thing my family had heard was that the course had ocean views, and would be the closest possible thing to Scottish-style golf. We loved watching the Open Championship on TV, dreaming of the idea of visiting the home of golf St Andrews, but this was different; this was in our backyard.

In those early days, Bandon was just the Lily Pond cottages and the main lodge. No separate golf shop, no pub and certainly none of the development you see today from Bandon Trails to Sheep Ranch. The driving range sat in the middle of the course – still my favourite set-up. At thirty-five dollars for the Oregonian Rate, it felt like we'd stumbled upon a secret. We just didn't know how big that secret would become.

After checking in just before sunset, we settled into a two-bedroom cottage and fuelled up on cheeseburgers. Ali and I shared one bed, our parents the other. That first round at Bandon remains vivid in my memory. My mother – who rarely walked golf courses with us – offered running commentary about our games. 'Ali needs to work on his putting!'; 'Akbar, you need to hit the ball over there, not there!'

The first hole threw us a curveball – we aimed for what we thought was the only green, only to discover there were two to choose from. Gorse-lined fairways guided us through holes 2 and 3, but there was still no sign of the promised ocean views. Then came the 4th, a narrow tunnel of fescue that finally revealed what all the fuss was about. As we rounded the dogleg, the sound of the Pacific growing louder with each step, the green seemed to vanish into the horizon where the ocean began. As we made our approach, the sound, the smell and the depth of the moment began to sink in. This was worth every minute of that four-and-a-half-hour drive.

2001

I returned to play the newly opened Pacific Dunes. My father had brought a business client, and word was that this new course was even better than the original. We could hardly imagine how that was possible, but imagination was all we had to go on. At the time, we barely had internet on dial-up, and there was none of the instant access to photography or swathes of 'golf content' that we have today.

This time, we drove down and back to Beaverton in a single day – nine hours of driving for one round of golf. It was worth it. Pacific Dunes was different from anything I'd ever seen in Oregon golf. While Bandon's fairways had been somewhat flattened, Pacific seemed to follow the natural contours of the land. Every mound, knoll and bunker looked like they'd simply planted grass on what was already there. At the turn stand, I found myself holding the largest chocolate chip cookie I'd ever seen, served by a pretty college-aged girl. So far, it seemed Bandon not only had great golf, but also the ladies. As a college student myself, this felt significant – though my assumption that 'Bandon had the ladies' would later be thoroughly disproven.

Cookie in hand, still processing what I'd seen, we walked down to the 4th. The view that appeared blew my mind – fairway and green perched along coastal cliffs, the Pacific stretching endlessly beyond. Every hole brought new surprises. The unconventional layout really hit home at the 9th – in Oregon, we never had blind tee shots, and here we were facing a hill with multiple possibilities. Not only was there no returning nine, but we were about to experience back-to-back par-3s, with the 11th quickly becoming my new favourite hole.

It was like listening to a complex piece of classical music or jazz – the varying circumstances forced you to be completely present, studying its design and strategy with all your senses. For an escapist like me, it was the perfect tonic – the wind howling, the visuals confounding, each shot demanding total commitment. Walking Pacific Dunes on an unpredictable Oregon day creates a rare meditative state.

The routing seemed to make the prevailing wind feel fair, even as it strengthened through our round. I played well, but more importantly, my mind was racing with possibilities. This resort had two incredible courses. Maybe the caddie shack was filled with gorgeous women? Oh, and cookies! Could I work here? Live here?

After the 18th hole, Ali and I parked our matching yellow Superman golf bags (ones we'd made for us and all our friends) and wandered into the shop, still buzzing from the experience. I asked the younger staff how they'd gotten their jobs – they'd all moved down for the summer to work. That's when Jim Wakeman appeared from the back and dropped his bombshell: 'You know, if you want a job, we can have you here working in guest services next week.'

The drive home was filled with encouragement from my dad and his client, Steve. 'Working at Bandon Dunes for the rest of the summer could be great,' they insisted.

'I'll talk to your mother, she will be fine. You need to do this,' my dad said. I called Amy Pendergast, an old friend who worked as lead merchandiser at Bandon. Her inflatable mattress in the guest room was available, and just days after my first round at Pacific, I was heading south to start my new job.

Amy's brother, Jesse, was out of town for a couple of weeks, so I inherited his inflatable mattress. My schedule was simple: morning shift from 5:30 am to 1:30 pm, then either pick up a caddie loop or wait for the 1st tee to open up. Sometimes I'd play with guests, but mostly I'd meet other employees and caddies for rounds.

Within days, I called my best friend, Forbes, the only person I knew who was even crazier about golf than me. He was about to have his final interview at Pizza Hut for a delivery job when I reached him. 'Fuck this, man. I'm gonna pack my shit and head down. Can you find me a job?' he said.

'Of course,' I replied, having no idea what I'd find him to do.

The next day I walked into General Manager Hank Hickox's office. 'I love working here and want to bring a friend or two down,' I said.

'Bring 'em all,' he replied. Now we just needed a place to stay.

The local Coffee Break advertiser led us to a recently renovated house with a monthly lease. The owner, Glen Rogie, looked exactly like Jerry Garcia and lived in the garage, where he had a small grow set-up. We never saw him for the entire time we lived there.

Forbes arrived, excited to see our new home. 'The outside isn't that pretty but he just redid the floors,' I told him. The floors were indeed new – a shiny laminate veneer – but that's where the luxury ended. Operating the washing machine required the use of a fork, but neither of us was mechanically inclined enough to master this art, so we'd trek to the laundromat next to Subway, where we went for our weekly treat nights. We slept on fold-out foam mats and within the first couple of days, one of us may or may not have clogged the toilet beyond repair. Forbes brought his microwave and we survived on hot pockets, trying every flavour and meticulously recording our ratings on the cardboard boxes for future reference.

2011 – Seamus Golf

Spending time in the shop at Bandon Dunes as a customer and employee led me to learn that the team had a culture of evolving the space and its vendors to best suit the golfers' needs. I learned so much about the golfers shopping there, and I believed that many would be interested in products that conveyed more of the story. For it to be such an authentic experience, it meant there were many ways to articulate a worthwhile message. If golf in Bandon was a representation of what golf is meant to be, and in many ways used to be, wouldn't the golfer shop for things that harkened the same sentiment?

With [my wife] Megan's experience at Pendleton, and lifelong appreciation of that brand, she knew a thing or two about a company that carried authenticity as a core value. Of all the things that Pendleton makes or has made in its storied history, it's the blankets that once formed a cultural ceremony for Native Americans and still are used in this same way today. The Bishop Family, owners of Pendleton, have only seen it one way – to find success and maintain the business from one generation to another because of their commitment to their figurative importance to such an integral part of American history.

When we began the business, we only used Pendleton wool, woven here in the Pacific Northwest, and made headcovers for Bandon Dunes. This was our best homage to the Scottish golf story, wherein local mills weave tartan and sew shops craft goods for sale at places like the home of golf, St Andrews.

While not a business idea yet, it became our passion and we grew the business to focus on golf experiences that exude authenticity. While Bandon Dunes was and continues to be the first of its kind, many great things for golf came from it. Chiefly, an opportunity to develop golf in other parts of the country and even the world. Starting our business in 2011, we followed the inquiries that came from golfers playing at Bandon Dunes. In the ensuing years, golf shops started selling more accessories than just hats and towels, starting with our development of the links-inspired headcover and ball mark category at places like Chambers Bay, Streamsong, Cabot Links, Sand Valley, Tara Iti and others.

For thirteen years now, we have operated and grown this business in line with the impact Bandon Dunes has had on golf. Today, our biggest customers still come from Oregon and its surrounding states. Because of Bandon's commitment to the locals, a different golfer has evolved, one who seeks to connect with the game at a deeper level. It's possible that the congregation of golf brands budding from the area, like Jones, MacKenzie Golf Bags and LAB Golf, simply had access to golfers of the future, who had tied their favourite experience to only the most important bucket list destination: Bandon Dunes.

The Future

My commitment to Bandon started with the decision at nineteen to start working there, buy a place and bring everybody I knew there. With that, my life would evolve but never stray far from that core idea. Culturally, I never felt more at home than when in Bandon. The people of the town were always so incredible, and still to this day, I often fantasise about being a bigger part of this community again and to give it back what it deserves. I find the types of people working there to be more relatable than any I've met in the broader world of golf. Many come from humble backgrounds and have a decisive commitment to the game that means committing their lives to it – both professionally and personally.

Golf provides a bounty to those who can taste the tonic it offers. Alister MacKenzie once said that he'd often prescribe golf to patients for many conditions ranging from anxiety and depression to 'general pain'. It would be impossible to argue that as a good remedy after spending an afternoon on the links of Bandon Dunes.

'Golf provides a bounty to those who can taste the tonic it offers.'

RANGES

WORDS AND PHOTOGRAPHY
BY BRYN DONKERSLOOT

In Wim Wenders' *Tokyo-Ga* (1985), the director explored the towering netted driving ranges dotting the city and noted: '... I was amazed by the degree to which [golf] was practiced here as pure form, as beauty and perfection of motion. The real aim of the game, to get the ball into a hole, seemed totally abandoned.'

XXIO
Victoria Golf
golf matters
DyDo
Audi西東京
150
140
120
110
100
30
30

The driving ranges found across the giant megalopolises of Japan and South Korea are the result of cities that boomed in population and filled any empty space before their discovery of golf, pushing courses beyond the perimeter and leaving inhabitants with a significant commute, impossible for most. This leaves millions of golfers with only the ranges (or now the popular golf simulators), and many may never play a proper course. These spaces often incorporate imitations of elements of the real thing, with painted-on greens and hazards between the golfer and the back netting, which may only be twenty metres. It feels different when you land in the white of a bunker and the ball bounces high off the concrete underneath. They vary in size, from only a few to hundreds of metres long; in location, from the tops of high-rise buildings to narrow mountainous valleys; in design, from completely plain to smart and heavily decorated; and in form, from small family-run businesses to large members-only gyms.

I first came across the concept for this project while flicking through Instagram, seeing a golfer's swing video in Ulsan, South Korea. Looking over the artificial grass-covered flooring and through the netting to the high-rise residential towers beyond, the way the range sat within the city intrigued me. I wanted to see what golf (and, more broadly, recreation as a whole) looked like in and around these dense urban environments.

8 0
8 0

동강병원
중앙건진센터

35
35
25
25

7

THE ROYAL BURN BACK

WORDS AND PHOTOGRAPHY
BY WILLIAM WATT

Every year, in the late summer or autumn, when the winds fall still, The Royal Melbourne ground staff swap their mowers for blowtorches. With careful planning, incredible precision and years of experience, the heathland areas at The Royal Melbourne receive a much-needed burn, providing long-awaited growth opportunities for some of the rarest and most delicate flora found anywhere in Australia.

'The indigenous heathland has always been part of the character of the courses here. We can see some history in the club records in the 1950s, where they used burning as a management tool. So it has a long history. But in the last fifteen or twenty years we have been using it more systematically each year, doing cyclical burns on specific areas on about a seven- to eight-year cycle.'

'It's very important in terms of keeping that balance between playability and keeping the vegetation there. We find it's a very important tool to keep those areas in the best condition possible.'

RICHARD FORSYTH, THE ROYAL MELBOURNE GOLF CLUB, DIRECTOR OF COURSES

'The site is typically prepared a month beforehand. So that gives an opportunity for the fuel that we use, which is just purely our own cuttings from other areas, to dry out. This helps us to get a good hot fire, because we want more heat rather than smoke in our burns. If it's wet or it's a more green material, you don't get the heat that you're after in the fire. Then it's always about tracking the weather leading up into that period where we're allowed to burn – we look for fairly close to still wind conditions.'

'We start by lighting a little small patch to see how the fire behaves. Even though you might think the wind is still, there might just be enough of a breeze to really kick it along. So just light a little bit first to see how the fire's reacting and then we can say, well nice and slow and we can light a few other areas up to get the fire moving and through the process. So once one area is burnt through, we don't let it just keep lingering on – we put it out straight away. We get the guys on the hoses to start watering behind the fire after it's been burning for five to ten minutes and then keep moving along. That way we're limiting the impact on the environment around us as well and trying to limit the smoke as best we can.'

‘What we’re doing with the burn by pretty much burning everything back down to ground level, it’s giving an opportunity for all the plants that are existing in that area to have their moment in the sun. Over a sustained period of years of just manually cutting back, the vegetation can become quite woody, especially at the base. That also then smothers sunlight to the lower growing plants underneath. So by removing those thicker bushy plants, it gives those undergrowth plants the chance to have their moment in the sun before it gets all dense and bushy again.’

STUART MOODIE, THE ROYAL MELBOURNE GOLF CLUB, HORTICULTURE FOREMAN

BARNBOUGLE AT EIGHTEEN

TASMANIA, AUSTRALIA

WORDS BY WILLIAM WATT
IN CONVERSATION WITH TOM DOAK,
BRIAN SCHNEIDER AND MIKE CLAYTON

PHOTOGRAPHY BY WILLIAM WATT
AND DAVE CARSWELL

As it celebrates its 18th birthday, we delve into the history and development of the remarkable Barnbougle Dunes. Through conversations with Tom Doak, Brian Schneider and Mike Clayton, we explore the challenges faced during construction, the natural changes over the years and the impact Barnbougle has had on golf, both in Australia and internationally.

'You do realise you're lucky to be playing golf at all at the moment, right?'

It's not the first time this has been suggested to me this week, usually from fathers much more experienced than I in the time pressures of looking after small children. At eight weeks, my son, Winston, is likely one of the younger travellers out on the golf tourism circuit at the moment, but so far, he seems to be enjoying it. Thankfully, life at Barnbougle, on Tasmania's northern coastline, seems to suit him. It helps that his mum, my wife Rosie, is amazingly relaxed, organised and supportive of a lifestyle that can involve early alarms, remote travel and long periods of Dad disappearing over the dunes in search of golf balls or photographs. Winston, after an initial six-week burst of seemingly insatiable energy and appetite, also seems to be turning into a pretty relaxed character. Our flatmates in the four-bedroom villa that overlooks the 1st fairway commented that they've barely heard a peep from him, despite our concerns that his late-night screaming sessions might disturb their precious pre-golf sleep.

The natural contours of the 17th at Barnbougle Dunes

Upon opening in December 2004, Barnbougle Dunes was unlike anything Australian golf had seen. A bold, rugged, naturalist course with a strict walking-only mantra and open to all the elements that nearby Bass Strait could throw at it. It would have been unlikely to see it built anywhere in that time, let alone perched on the coast near the remote town of Bridport in what was then considered sleepy Tasmania. What seems like a raging success and a natural use of this land today was certainly not assured or inevitable at the time. Much like a human birth, the early days of a golf course aren't for the faint-hearted – the risk levels are high, the unknowns are many and it certainly helps to be in good hands. Which, fortunately for Australian golf, Barnbougle definitely was. Greg Ramsay encouraged Mike Clayton (who was working with John Sloane and Bruce Grant under MCGD at the time) to be a local guide for Tom Doak, who was extremely enthusiastic about the site. Still hesitant, landowner Richard Sattler met with Mike Keiser, whose revolutionary Bandon Dunes was really starting to take off, for some encouragement on the viability of the idea as a business. Again, enthusiasm abounded and the Barnbougle Dunes project took off.

Barnbougle has matured into a reliable staple of the Australian golf circuit for locals, mainlanders and international visitors alike. Any Aussie who seeks a deeper appreciation of the game than the occasional weekend whack around at the local has either been here, or is planning to come here one day.

The timing of our trip of early autumn has meant the ferocious winds that can hit the courses have been entirely absent this week (except for an epic storm on day five, which caused me to abandon the round on the 11th fairway). This relative calm – both in the conditions and on a personal level – has allowed me to get to know the place a little better. And I think Barnbougle knows itself a little better these days. It's a place comfortable in its own skin, having gone through the fledgling early years as a rambunctious only child, before being joined by a sibling in 2010 with the more restrained twenty-hole Lost Farm course being added. More recently a third course, the wildly fun fourteen-hole Bougle Run, has joined the stable. This has perhaps completed the Barnbougle family, although there are always whispers of another course around these parts.

To gain an appreciation for how the course has matured over the years, we spoke with co-designers Tom Doak and Mike Clayton, and lead shaper on the project, Brian Schneider, about the genesis of the project and how it has changed in the decades since. From speaking with these three key figures about the design and construction of the course, it becomes clear how fondly the course is thought of in their minds, and contrastingly how much of a gamble it felt like at the time the project first came to fruition.

Tom Doak

How did you originally become involved in the Barnbougle Dunes project?

Tom Doak: Greg Ramsay contacted me about it in 2001. I was busy, but my associate Bruce Hepner was making a trip to Australia, so I asked him to go and see the land and meet Greg. Bruce and Mike Clayton went together, and said it had the right stuff, although they struggled to understand the scale of the property and whether it was big enough for the course. So I asked Greg for topo[graphic] maps to start working on potential routings. I actually visited the site for the first time and met Greg in June of 2002, with Clayts and my son, Michael, who was eleven at the time, tagging along. One of my memories of my first visit is having lunch at the Sattlers' house with Michael and all of Richard's kids who were mostly young teens. It was pretty hard to imagine then how important the project would be to his family, or that Penny would wind up being the GM of a substantial resort!

What are some of the most dramatic changes you have noticed to the Barnbougle Dunes course since its opening in 2004, both naturally occurring and through deliberate adjustments?

TD: Unfortunately, I don't get back that often to check on progress. The two biggest changes I've seen are the shrinking of the 7th green – it has been eroding into the bunker at the left over time – and the loss of dunes to the right of the tee shot on 17. They used to redig the cut straight out to the ocean every couple of years, but I don't think they are doing it anymore, and the wind is forming a sandbar off Sally's Point that makes the water cut back against the dunes on the 17th. There isn't much buffer left between that fairway and the ocean!

To what extent did you try to mitigate the future natural evolution of the course, versus embracing it, at the time of construction?

TD: We built the course on a very tight budget, so we sort of had to embrace the natural evolution of things.

The underrated par-4 3rd hole at Barnboulge Dunes

The famous bunker of the 4th has become even more dramatic over time – why does this occur and is it possible for it to become too intimidating?

TD: Wind erosion is a fact of life in those big sprawling bunkers golfers love – that's why they are called 'blowouts'. All you can do is replace sand, or break up the bunker into smaller pieces that will erode less. But everyone loves that big bunker, so we haven't been asked to change it yet.

How much of a statement was the 7th, Tom's Little Devil, at the time of construction? How has this hole evolved over the eighteen years since the build?

TD: It's funny that the hole is named after me, because that's probably the one hole that Mike Clayton had the most to do with. The original 7th was going to play more to the north, but Brian, Mike and I all felt that would be an impossible shot in the left-to-right crosswind, so Mike suggested turning the hole back into the wind, and I knew where that green site was from an earlier routing attempt. My friend Tim Weiman had always talked about how much he liked those 'little devil' par-3 holes so that's where the name actually came from.

What are some of the signs that a golf course is maturing well? Are there any courses in your portfolio that you feel have aged particularly well/poorly?

TD: My old friend Dave Wilber, who was turf consultant for Pacific Dunes and Barnbougle, once said that if an architect's courses are like his kids, then the greenkeeper is the guy we want our daughter to marry. They are really the ones who are going to take care of our baby long term. It's going to evolve – either for the better, or for the worse. We've been lucky at Barnbougle to have Phil Hill as the superintendent since it opened and he has certainly guided it towards the former. In fact, generally, the places where the superintendent we originally worked with is still in charge are evolving best: Pacific Dunes, Streamsong and Tara Iti come to mind. By contrast, my original client at High Pointe went through six or seven superintendents over twenty years before the course closed.

Is there a 'peak age' for a golf course in terms of balancing the designer's intent and what evolves over time?

TD: It really depends on the place. Places like Bandon and Barnbougle are so dynamic in terms of the weather that I don't think you can afford to fall in love with what it looks like at any given point. When we do get to rebuilding the 7th green at Barnbougle, we will have to overbuild it, because it will just start eroding again the moment we are finished.

What impact do you think Barnbougle Dunes has had on golf in Australia and internationally?

TD: Mike Keiser took an interest in the project as a case study. He figured if a resort could be successful in as remote a place as Tasmania, the model would work in a lot of other places, too. So, it really confirmed for him that the success of Bandon Dunes was not a one-off, if you got certain parts of the model right. Certainly, in Australia, Barnbougle helped to prove that golfers would travel to play a true links course, and Richard Sattler's willingness to stick his neck out and develop it has spawned several other projects that now compete with the original.

Are there changes that you would love to see happen with the course over the next eighteen years?

TD: I'd like to move it closer to home, but sadly that is not possible.

Brian Schneider

How did you first become involved in the project, and what were your first impressions of the site?

Brian Schneider: We were nearing the end of our project at Cape Kidnappers in New Zealand when Tom first made me aware of the potential project in Tasmania. All of Tom's team – Bruce Hepner, Brian Slawnik and Eric Iverson – were involved at CK and we had basically set up shop there for the better part of a year. That was only my second project with Tom, so I was the new guy in the group and the more senior associates were ready to head home after a long time away. Moving on to another project in that part of the world didn't much appeal to them, but I was enjoying that time on the road and when Tom showed me a few pics of the Barnbougle property, I was all in.

We made a trip to Tassie a month or so later and I was absolutely blown away. The opportunity to work in coastal dunes right on the beach seemed too good to be true. It was as beautiful as any site I'd ever seen, and I couldn't believe I was getting the opportunity to work in such a place.

How remote did Barnbougle feel at the time of construction? Travelling to the course today is relatively easy, and to an extent it has put Bridport on the map. But I imagine in 2004 this must have seemed like a long way from anywhere.

BS: It's still a long way from home but it certainly felt like the end of the world at that time. I think that's part of its appeal. In reality, it's a very easy (and affordable) trip from much of mainland Australia, which has been important to its success. It's a very popular destination for Australians and an easy add-on for international golfers making the trek to play the great courses of Melbourne and Sydney.

Are there any holes that stand out in your mind as being particularly interesting to construct?

BS: In my mind, there are essentially two basic hole types: those that are found and those that are built. Barnbougle is blessed with a high number of the former. Some of those holes came together very quickly and a few of the greens are almost entirely as we found them. The wild contours of the putting surfaces on the par-3 13th and par-4 17th, for example, are largely natural. The 4th, 7th and 15th are other favourites that took relatively little effort to shape.

The short par-4 12th fell on the other end of the spectrum. The entire hole was carved out of a high dune ridge and had to be rebuilt several times as it repeatedly blew away in the strong Tassie winds. It's always been one of my favourite holes on the course but despite taking up a small slice of the property, it was probably the most difficult one to get in the ground.

What were some of the biggest challenges faced during construction?

BS: Building golf in seaside dunes is extraordinarily fun, but the aforementioned wind was a constant foe and made for some pretty miserable working conditions on our worst weather days. The soft beach sand is prone to wind erosion, and shaped features are quickly wiped out when a gale rolls in. Most of the greens, bunkers and fairway contours had to be rebuilt many times.

Any time you're working in an area as remote as Bridport, finding labour to build the course is a challenge. Nonetheless, we were able to assemble a terrific crew of locals to install irrigation and get the course grassed. They took a lot of pride in creating something special for their community and some of them are still Barnbougle employees two decades on.

How did you find working with the local community as excitement grew around the project?

BS: I don't think any of us quite knew just what the place would become, and it's such a pleasure to get back to Barnbougle now to see how it continues to grow and evolve. The Sattlers are truly wonderful people and I couldn't be happier for their success. It was a giant leap of faith on their part and their all-in commitment – along with the deep involvement of the local community – made it as enjoyable and rewarding as any project I've ever experienced.

To what extent did you try to mitigate or embrace the natural changes to the course that were likely to occur over the years?

BS: It didn't take long to realise that what we built was going to evolve quickly. Mother Nature is a powerful force and it's best to embrace change because fighting it is futile.

Areas of exposed sand are most susceptible to wind erosion. With that in mind, we tried to minimise the number of bunkers and to locate them in places where their evolution wouldn't have a negative impact on the playing experience. There are relatively few greenside bunkers at Barnbougle and many are intentionally positioned at a slight remove from the putting surface so that blowing sand would be unlikely to alter hole locations.

You also learn quickly that getting too attached to the look of what you build is bound to cause some grief. A bunker may look great the day it's grassed but by opening day, the details you'd spent hours refining have been completely wiped away. In all cases, things evolve towards a more natural aesthetic. In that sense, our work is constantly being passively improved.

What are some of the most significant changes you have noticed as the course has matured? Are there any nice surprises in this respect?

BS: The best element of the natural evolution of any course is probably the maturation of its turf. Barnbougle has benefited greatly from having just a small handful of head greenkeepers in its lifetime and they've always done an extraordinary job of presenting authentic links conditions.

The course plays exactly as you'd hope, offering the opportunity to play a wide variety of shots and allowing you to succeed with any style of play. The course was designed to embrace and even encourage the ground game and its greenkeeping staff have beautifully married the proper conditions to its contours.

How does Barnbougle compare with some of the other world-class projects you have worked on?

BS: As the first project on which I served as lead associate for Tom, Barnbougle will always be a special place to me. It's also a really fun golf course and I can honestly say there's nowhere in the world I'd rather play.

Mike Clayton

How did you first get involved in the project? And what were your first impressions of the site when you did make it down there?

Mike Clayton: We walked over the site, and obviously it was great. And as we left the site, Bruce said of Greg Ramsey, 'I've met that kid a hundred times. He always gives you that "I'll make you famous" speech. It'll never happen.' It was probably a pretty good assessment of where things were at, at the time.

Then Tom came down, within a year or so, and met Richard. Tom went back and spoke to Mike Keiser about it, who then came out, saw the land and told Richard that he should do it. He took Richard to Bandon, showed him how that worked, and told the GM at Bandon that, 'Richard's here for a week, your job's to teach him everything I know.' So Richard was there for a week, saw how that worked, got some investors in and went ahead with building the golf course.

It was incredibly unusual to find somebody who didn't play golf, didn't know anything about it, who was prepared to commit to such a big project. The brief for the clubhouse to the architect was, 'If the course goes broke and no one turns up to play it, I want to be able to turn the clubhouse into my family home and we'll just go and live in it.'

Tom and I thought it would work because we knew how good the golf course could be. And Mike Keiser thought it would work from a business perspective, knowing how Bandon was operating. Everyone else I spoke to thought it was completely mad. 'No one will ever go down and play there. The weather's shit, it's in the middle of nowhere' and so on. But they'd never seen the land, so they had no clue as to how good the course was going to be.

At that time, Bridport was not really known at all. Barnbougle has put it on the map to an extent.

MC: Bridport was a little sleepy fishing village where the population swelled up in the summertime. It was a nice little town. We enjoyed it. But it wasn't exactly ... there was the top pub and the bottom pub, they were the only two places to eat. In a sense, Barnbougle became another local restaurant as well. It's been great for the locals. Barnbougle is the biggest employer in north-east Tasmania now.

Can you talk me through that routing process and how long it took and how many iterations you went through?

MC: Tom had done some stuff on the contour maps and he had a rough idea of what he wanted to do. The first routing he had, the 10th hole was a great hole. It was from out the front of the clubhouse going backwards up the 18th. And then you played the 11th hole inland up a big valley behind what's now the 13th tee. There were holes backwards down today's 14th and 15th, and the last two holes were today's 11th and 10th in reverse. So it was very different. Mike Keiser came out and said, 'No, you've got to finish with the holes coming down the beach,' which was exactly right. So he was a big contributor to the back nine routing. It basically got flipped after that comment.

Looking at the front nine, the 7th stands out today as a unique and memorable hole. Was it always planned that way?

MC: No. We went out there with Brian Schneider because he was down there a lot of the time and had a good feel for the site. We stood in the tee and Tom pointed one finger to where the green is now and another ninety degrees to the right, playing straight towards the ocean, which would've been a much shorter walk to the next tee. 'Where do we go? Which one?' and Brian and I both said, 'That one,' which is the one that got built.

The green site was basically sitting there, which was probably why we picked it. The other one would've been better in terms of the routing, but would've been a massive crosswind hole, which would've been really tricky on a short par-3. So I think it was better going the way we did because at least it's straight into the wind, which is difficult but more playable than it would've been in a crosswind. I guess we could have built both of them, which would've been interesting.

When you were first looking and building the course, did you try to mitigate some of the natural changes that were likely to occur? Or did you just embrace the fact that was likely to happen?

MC: I played with Ben Crenshaw at Sand Hills one year and he said, 'It's amazing, every time I come back here, the bunkers are different because of what the wind does to them.' It's the same at Barnbougle – the bunkers have changed, and some of them have changed a lot. The left-hand bunker at 14 has changed a lot, and there's that big mound there when you come off the green.

The bunker on the left of 7 has changed a bit. Bits of the green fall into the bunker. But we didn't talk about it at the time. I guess if someone had said, 'Do you think the wind's going to change these bunkers?', the answer was probably, 'Yep.' But it was hard to predict which ones it would change and how it would change them. So it's just part of the evolution. It's not like it's gotten worse or better because of how the bunkers have changed. They've just changed because the wind changes them. And there's not really much you can do about it; it is just links golf really. The road hole bunker has changed over the years – it doesn't look anything like it used to. It's just part of the evolution of golf by the sea.

The good thing is there wasn't anything significant that needed to change. Like The Royal Melbourne and Kingston Heath, the best courses in the country, there's no need to change anything because everything got put in the right place to start with. It was a good routing. There's not one green site you would move, or a tee position you'd change because that'd be a better angle from over there. So it was testament to Tom and the quality of the routing that everything's in the right place.

It will be true at Seven Mile Beach as well. Everything's in the right place. Everything's in the right proportion. You nail the best green sites and you build good greens. As MacKenzie said – you finish up with finality, which is important because it just costs money in the end to change bad decisions. But it's amazing how many times you see it happen.

Is there a whole or section of the course that you particularly enjoy going back to?

MC: Not really. I think it's all good. The 4th is obviously a great short par-4 to play. I like the 6th, and it's a really cool shot into 7. The 15th is good. If you are going to mark them from 1 to 18, maybe 16 would be the last one. Most people would probably pick the 2nd after that, but I think the 2nd is a really good hole. It's a great green, it's an interesting hole. It just happens to be on flat ground.

It's like most people would pick the 17th at Port Fairy as being the worst hole. But if you put the ocean on the right-hand side of it, they'd pick the same hole as being the best hole. Because they're not actually judging the hole, they're judging the ambiance of the hole, and the holes that come before it. Because they're all in the ocean, they get to 17 and think, 'Well, this hole isn't very good.' So I think the 2nd gets criticised by some people because it's the only hole on the flat ground. But aside from that, I think people would have a wildly different perception of what the next least-good hole was.

Some might pick the 8th because they can't get up the cliff. So they've got to lay it up and then face a blind pitch up the hill. But for a long hitter, it's just a really good, strong hole downwind. For some people, that's a controversial hole, but people need to face a proper challenge when they get out there – that is ultimately why people keep going back there to play.

The most important thing was to build something that would be a viable business that wasn't going to send Richard broke. It was important to build holes that people enjoyed playing, and build a sequence of holes that meant people were going to come back and play it. There are projects that get screwed up because they don't get to their potential. It would've been no good going down there building a seven out of ten – that would've gone broke. It had to be a nine out of ten for it to work. It was the same with Lost Farm and it's the same with Seven Mile Beach. To make these things work, they've got to be fantastic, to have people get on a plane and go to Hobart or go to Launceston just to play golf. The promise has got to be that the golf at the other end will be great. It has to be in The Royal Melbourne/Kingston Heath class, otherwise it's just not going to work.

What do you think the impact of Barnbougle has been on Australian golf and future projects such as Seven Mile?

MC: Seven Mile Beach wouldn't have happened if it wasn't for Barnbougle. And Barnbougle wouldn't have happened if it wasn't for Bandon. And Bandon probably wouldn't have happened if it wasn't for Sand Hills. So there's a direct line between all those. Sand Hills showed that remote golf could work. Bandon showed that remote public golf would work.

But why it's important and why I think Richard is in the top-five most important people in Australian golf ever: because for the first time in Australia someone built a top-100 course in the world that everyone could play. Sure, if you know someone you can get on at The Royal Melbourne, Kingston Heath, Royal Adelaide or New South Wales. They're certainly more accessible than the equivalent clubs in the Unites States. But for the first time, every and any Australian could play a top-100 course. That's why it was so important.

The irony is that Richard didn't play golf. Didn't play golf, didn't know anything about it really. There have been a lot of people who could have afforded to do what he did, who played golf, but didn't do it for whatever reason. But it took a non-golfer to do something as important as Barnbougle – you wouldn't want to put a bet on that ever happening.

Barnbougle has led to Lost Farm, which is another top-100 course, Cape Wickham and now Seven Mile Beach, which is likely to be. So it's possibly spawned four top-100 courses in the world, all in Tasmania. It's great for tourism, it's great for Tasmania. Tasmania's got a phenomenal climate for golf. I think you could make the argument that it's got the best climate in the world for golf, because you can play all year and because you can grow fescue. And fescue's the ultimate grass to play golf on. It's just the perfect surface to play off. Fescue is cashmere and couch is lambswool.

Postscript

It's day four at Barnbougle, and with all our coverage for Seed Golf wrapped up, we're able to treat ourselves to a camera-free round, playing from the tips on The Dunes course in perfectly still conditions. I'm acutely aware of how days like this must be savoured, having just listened to a stream of fatherhood podcasts. One of the episodes that stuck in my mind was a dad talking about a moment where he was sleepily eating cereal with one hand while cradling his baby in the other – a fairly typical juggling act of a new parent. He had wondered how many times he might experience this type of moment. Even if it happened a few times a week, his conclusion was it would be maybe twenty or thirty times before his child was too big to be held in such a way. Then that was it. Forever.

Suddenly, a routine moment of eating breakfast with the added challenge of cradling a child became something so precious that he welled up just talking about it.

I had applied it to the very early days of fatherhood as well, realising that the seemingly interminable 3 am wakeups would one day be just a blip in my life. That the tickles, the giggles, the pram naps, the feeds and yes, even the spit ups – all of it was so fleeting. Before long, I realised that everything in life is just as fleeting. It all happens only once.

Golf, as always, is a great metaphor for life. We never hit the same golf shot twice. We'll probably never play in this exact foursome again, especially as the 1st tee time on a still day at Barnbougle. And even if we do, this will be one of only a handful of times in our entire life. It's a little daunting to think about it that way – what if I top it off the 1st tee? But it is also a beautiful mindset to be in. It makes you want to breathe it all in as deeply as possible.

As we emerge from the shady teeing grounds into the warming sun of the 1st fairway, with a solid drive in play, I glance back at our accommodation, bunkered into the dunes above. Rosie is waving down at us smiling with Winston cradled in her other arm. *Wow. I guess that'll only happen once.*

I struggle to hit my second shot, peering through the tears in my eyes, and top it into the fairway bunker. I'm not bothered, though – it has never been more obvious to me that the score is irrelevant. Being here is all that matters. 'Lucky' doesn't even begin to describe it.

FROM PIXELS TO PUTTS

WORDS AND PHOTOGRAPHY
BY LUKAS MICHEL

'At these older courses, there seems to be a broader acceptance of extreme features that would be objected to on a modern course.'

Amid the ever-evolving world of technology, the realm of golf course architecture has experienced its own transformation, with digital tools reshaping the design process and the way we interact with the natural beauty of these landscapes. Tom Doak's precise recreation of the Lido course at Sand Valley has opened a window to the bold designs of eras past. Lukas Michel asks: is modern golf design being too safe?

The Evolution of Golf Course Design in the Digital Era

Nestled among the suburbs of growing cities or in popular vacation spots lie timeless gems of golf course design. Here, legendary architects – including Alister MacKenzie, Harry Colt and Donald Ross – applied their creativity like master craftsmen and etched their names in the annals of golf architecture history. However, creating this legacy wasn't an easy endeavour. Just as US President Woodrow Wilson described golf as a game that used 'weapons singularly ill-designed for the purpose', golf course construction technologies in this era limited the creative expression of these geniuses.

Over the last thirty years or so, we have been lucky to witness a renaissance in the theory of golden age golf course design and, coupled with modern-day construction methods, new names have emerged to carry the torch of golf architecture and guide it into the future. When playing the modern designs of Tom Doak, Gil Hanse, Mike DeVries or Bill Coore, I often find myself asking a question that feels a little taboo: are all those great classic courses really any better than this?

Modern architects benefit from a growing resource of information and an abundance of living examples of great golf architecture, so it stands to reason that they should be more educated in golf course design than those who came before. Rather than having to rely on limited literature or long journeys by boat or train, modern architects have the books of MacKenzie, Hunter,

Simpson and Doak; and hundreds of revered courses just a short plane trip or drive away.

Additionally, we have a plethora of other information available at our fingertips. A quick search of any course reveals Google Earth images and topographical maps, which can be used to study the best courses and understand what makes them great. For instance, a 4K drone flyover and LiDAR scan of the 4th hole on the Old Course is available in mere seconds if we want to visualise the exact scale and shape to the famous bump in front of its green.

These same technologies aid immensely in the design and construction of golf courses. Historically, architects would need weeks or months to find the ideal layout for a new site. However, these architects were often limited to a few days of walking the property, inevitably resulting in suboptimal course routings. Then, while building greens, slopes were eyeballed and rudimentary techniques used to ensure surface drainage and playing interest. By contrast, the modern architect can use detailed topographical and geological surveys of a large site to quickly identify the desired areas to build golf. Afterwards, they can traverse the site quickly with an ATV to map out the ideal routing. Finally, when shaping and finishing a green, it can be quickly surveyed using a drone or rover unit to check for surface drainage and pinnable area.

All this is without considering the earthmoving equipment at the disposal of modern-day designers. Anyone visiting The Royal Melbourne will have driven past the horse-drawn scoop and plough on the entrance drive. These rudimentary tools were used to construct all thirty-six green complexes of the East and West courses. It's difficult to imagine the hours Morcom, Russell and their crew spent meticulously shaving contours to achieve their and MacKenzie's joint vision of perfection. By comparison, while working on the Seven Mile Beach project in Hobart, we used bulldozers, an excavator and dump truck to carry out the bulk of the earthmoving in a fraction of the time it would have taken in MacKenzie's era. On the 3rd and 4th holes, where the natural terrain was too dramatic for golf, we moved around 50,000 cubic metres of sand in just a few weeks to create playable areas from unreasonably steep dunes. In the past, the routing may have avoided this land altogether, but at Seven Mile Beach, these two holes will be genuine highlights.

However, even this amount of earthmoving pales in comparison to other modern designs. While working as a construction supervisor on Tom Fazio's ambitious design at Hudson National, Mike DeVries recalls the stunning sight and sound of clearing 100,000 cubic metres of rock using explosives alone. Several years later, when DeVries had his opportunity to build a course on a similar site in Marquette, Michigan, he made a point of designing to minimise environmental disruption. Skilfully routed through dramatic terrain and metamorphic rock, the aptly named Greywalls course at Marquette Golf Club is spectacular, with several holes using exposed rock as strategic features or stunning backdrops. Of course, modern earthmoving capabilities were still used on this difficult property. Indeed, much of the front nine was sand-capped and shaped with material transported from the back nine, but the design and construction work are indistinguishable from the natural terrain. Tom Fazio's and Mike DeVries' respective designs, although different in style and construction philosophy, show the capabilities of modern construction techniques to create playable courses on extreme properties. With all these modern tools and technologies, how is it possible that just five of the world's top fifty courses in GOLF.com's latest rankings were built after 1940? Data available from the United States shows that approximately 3,000 golf courses existed by 1940, with more than 10,000 added since. The numbers don't seem to add up. The simple answer is that almost all of those 10,000-plus golf courses genuinely aren't as good as the earlier courses. Paradoxically, the problems with many of the modern courses are due to the new tools, technologies and the architects themselves. Since modern earthmoving equipment enables the transport of huge quantities of dirt, the prevailing belief was that golf no longer needed to be situated on beautiful, undulating and free-draining terrain in order to be great. With clever design and modern technology, that could all be created, or so everyone thought. As housing demand pushed development away from the cities and into barren and soulless pastures, what better way to beautify a landscape and generate higher housing prices than by routing a golf course among a neighbourhood? And off the developers went, continuing largely unchecked until the housing crisis of 2008. This situation accounts for that incredible number of new – and primarily bad – golf courses designed in what some have called the 'dark age of golf design'.

The 4th hole at 7 Mile Beach after rough shaping – the land here was softened drastically to improve the playability of the hole.

'MacKenzie's attraction towards design features that look natural was that he could use the land as his scapegoat for bolder design work.'

With all that said, there have been a number of truly great courses built in the last thirty years or so. The modern names you've heard of – Sand Hills, Bandon Dunes, Friars Head, Tara Iti, Castle Stuart, Barnbougle – all share something in common: great land. Unlike the thousands of housing-development-style courses, the modern greats are all centred around outstanding golf sites. This all started with Richard 'Dick' Youngscap's development of Sand Hills Golf Club in remote Nebraska, and was further validated with Mike Keiser's Bandon Dunes and his later projects with Richard Sattler at Barnbougle, Ben Cowan-Dewar at Cabot Links, and his sons at Sand Valley. Others have copied this model, and they have all discovered there is indeed money to be made from pure golf, so long as it's good enough.

However, one further question remains: how do Pine Valley, Cypress Point, St Andrews and The Royal Melbourne consistently rate higher than anything built in the modern era? I'm not sure they should.

At historic and classic designs, I'm frequently shocked by the boldness of the architecture. This reflects the original spirit of the game, which had little reverence for modern expectations of 'fairness'. North Berwick's unpredictable and wildly contoured 16th green, Prestwick's blind par-3 5th hole up and over a dune, and (closer to my home) Woodlands' narrow and perched 4th green come to mind here. While walking off these holes I inevitably say to myself, 'good luck building that today!' At these older courses, there seems to be a broader acceptance of extreme features that would be objected to on a modern course. This has precisely unfolded at the Lakes Golf Club in Sydney, where Mike Clayton built a hole inspired by the aforementioned 4th at Woodlands. While some critics have praised it (Tom Doak included a photo of the hole in his *Confidential Guide to Golf Courses*), it has proven less popular with golfers, with the hole rumoured to be redesigned soon. Whether it's because the architects of historic courses are long passed ('don't speak ill of the dead') or there's an understanding of the limited technology at their disposal, there's a tendency to look past, or even praise quirks that may otherwise be highlighted as flaws in courses of the modern era.

This philosophical peculiarity reminds me of a quote from the remarkably prescient *Spirit of St Andrews* by Alister MacKenzie. When describing the construction of his course at Alwoodley, MacKenzie describes the goal of deceiving golfers 'into believing the artificial features we had made were by Nature,' which would allow him to 'get away with it and escape their hostile criticism'. Evidently, MacKenzie's attraction towards design features that look natural was that he could use the land as his scapegoat for bolder design work. In contrast, the difficulty the modern architect faces is the assumption that almost all of what is on the ground was either shaped or left in place with intent. The challenge of playing golf against the quirks of nature has been all but removed from the toolset of the contemporary designer.

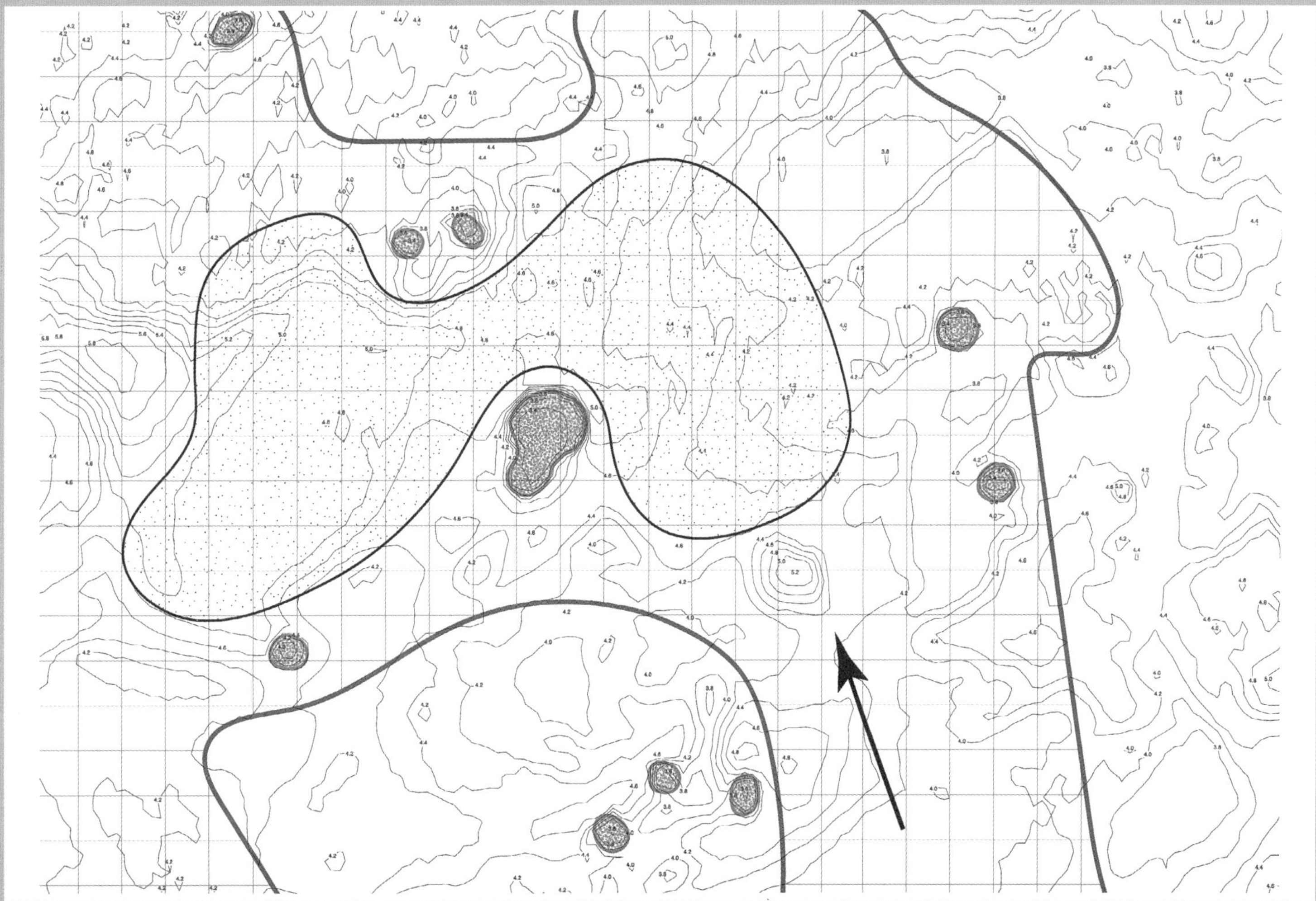

A 0.2m interval contour plan produced from a 2m resolution LiDAR scan of the 4th/14th greens at the Old Course of St Andrews. The arrow indicates the direction of play for the 4th hole, with its iconic bump indicated by the concentric contours near the head of the arrow and just short of the green. 5m grid squares.

Mike DeVries surveys his construction of the 13th green at Seven Mile Beach

The Lido

This all leads to the most confounding reaction to a golf course I've ever had. In late 2022, I was fortunate to have a preview look at Mike and Chris Keiser's recreation of the Lido Golf Club in Wisconsin – likely the most revered course to ever close. On this unique project, Tom Doak was enlisted to 'restore' the C B Macdonald masterpiece, eighty years after it shuttered and some 1000 miles from its original location. Using a combination of historic imagery, modern video-game software and state-of-the-art GPS construction technology, Doak and his team (notably Peter Flory, Brian Schneider and Brian Zager) have been able to produce a true replica of the original Long Island, New York, golf course. The design is bold and provocative, with a number of forced carries and ubiquitous, penal bunkering.

Like Macdonald, I studied at the University of St Andrews in Scotland, so could see the resemblance and inspiration from the famous Old Course, which I've played countless times. Despite this familiarity, I struggled to come to terms with the course. On one hand, I was seeing a golf course built in the modern era and viewed it with the baggage and expectations of modern golfers and modern design. On the other hand, this was an authentic recreation of a course from the early golden age, representative of its era and should be viewed as such. Initially, I thought many of the severe bunkers and contours at the Lido were exaggerated to account for changes in modern equipment, or even a mistake. Surely the course wasn't that hard, given the equipment the course was originally played with? However, in researching and understanding the length Doak's team went into ensuring the accuracy of the design and construction of the course, the mistake was on my part. I had underestimated the evolution and change in golfer expectations. Golf, in Macdonald's era, wasn't fair or predictable to appease the golfer trying to break their handicap. The game was a wildly difficult yet fun adventure, where the point was to beat your opponent, no matter how many strokes it took.

The Lido also provoked deeper thought about the state of modern golf course design. If The Royal Melbourne, Pine Valley and Cypress Point are yet to be unseated by a modern course, perhaps modern design is lacking something. Much like how good courses fit their topographical landscape, they also tend to fit their historical landscape. It is impossible to separate the story of a course's design from the factors surrounding its conception. Could the watered-down design preferences of present-day golfers be holding back golf course design?

I think so, but there are exceptions, with the very best of modern design still pushing the envelope. Barnbougle's 112-metre 7th hole, aptly named 'Tom Little Devil' (after Tom Doak, its co-designer) is one such example. The tiny 270-square-metre green – elevated and protected by gaping bunkers on the left and deep swales at the back and right – is a formidable target in the seaside winds. Even MacKenzie may have taken his foot off the proverbial accelerator here. Speaking of MacKenzie, six holes later, at the 13th, the putting surface is an homage to the good doctor's famous Sitwell Park green, which was bulldozed not long after its opening for being too severe. Thankfully, it lives on in spirit in north-east Tasmania.

Two hundred kilometres south of Barnbougle, at Seven Mile Beach, I'm curious to see the public's reaction to several holes that I think will challenge the 'fairness brigade'. The three par-3s that are grassed thus far – 2, 14 and 17 – all present as challenging targets, despite a total of two bunkers across the three holes. While hitting balls on a recent site visit, it took me four shots to hit the 14th hole in regulation (a downhill 170-metre par-3). I was left with several demanding pitch shots from within and around the sharp marram-covered dunes that eat into the putting surface like no other hole I've ever seen.

Ultimately, the challenge for golf course architects moving forward is to take advantage of current and future technical innovation and respond to golfer expectations and tastes, while respecting the spirit of the game and its origins. It's a fine balance, but the truly great courses of golden age design have proven able to transcend changes in the game and remain as the most inspiring examples of great golf. I think future design work could better showcase the original spirit of the game and respect the architects that set the stage for golf, as the very best courses of the modern era – Sand Hills, Barnbougle and Friars Head – have. Whether these contemporary classics can take their place in the very top echelon of golf design will only be answered with time.

My bet is they do.

9

BREAKING BAD AT BONDI

SYDNEY, AUSTRALIA

WORDS AND PHOTOGRAPHY
BY ADRIAN LOGUE

Overlooking the world-famous Bondi Beach is the distinctly not famous Bondi Golf & Diggers Club. Running along stunning clifftops, this nine-hole public golf course takes some of the most expensive real estate in the world, yet offers a truly accessible golf experience.

'Wear what's comfortable for you – there are no restrictions on the course.'

Is there a more subversive sentence in golf? And yet those dozen words are the complete dress regulations for Bondi Golf & Diggers Club. Words have power, and golf's normal dress rules consist of words with the power to turn people away, to deny access, to shame and humiliate. Formidable words like 'collared shirt', 'dress pants', 'pleated fronts', 'capris' and 'skort'.

Such words hold back the barbarians at golf's gate and protect its homogeneity. Dress rules are words that fit with golf's message: *we welcome you and your diversity ... if it conforms to our institutional rules.*

And so to Bondi's unusual dress code. They're the sort of dangerous words that raise a surfboard-waxed middle finger at golf's appropriately dressed establishment. Simple words, devoid of jargon, completely unambiguous and written by a real human.

But do these words 'grow the game' with what is the traditionally 'right' sort of golfer? I, for one, hope not. So I grab my camera and head to Sydney's eastern suburbs on a crisp autumn afternoon in search of diversity and stories among the untraditional rabble crawling over Bondi's welcoming fairways.

No sooner do I arrive at Bondi than I meet a fella named Mick. Mick is hunched over an impossible chip, short-sided off hard pan, semi-blind up a hill to a tiny disc of green. I am at least as surprised as Mick when he clips his ball off the dirt, lands it gently on the fringe and stops it next to the pin.

'Did you fuckin' see that!?' he shouts to his mate Jimmy. (Jimmy hadn't seen a fuckin' thing, because Jimmy was struggling with his fifth fuckin' chip up on the other side of the fuckin' green.)

I ask to take their photo after they hole out. 'It's for an article I'm writing about public golf at Bondi,' I say.

'No problem, mate,' Mick said. 'Did you see that fuckin' shot I hit?'

I assure him I definitely had. Mick puffs his chest in his cotton hoodie, adjusts his nylon trucker hat and swaggers to the next tee. I notice a pretty persimmon wood among his beaten-up, mismatched clubs.

'That's a nice driver you've got there,' I remark.

'That thing?' He snorts. 'I got all these clubs at the council cleanup. The bag and buggy too. Someone just left them on the nature strip!' Mick's total outlay to get started with golf was approximately zero dollars, give or take.

Mick and Jimmy are clutching stubby holders cooling cans of Bondi Beach Beer, a tasty drop from a local craft brewery. In fact, almost every group I encounter has stubby holders and a supply of cans in their bags. In addition to its cooling properties, the stubby holder gives one's can a nice wide base to help it stay upright on the ground while hitting a shot.

I follow Mick and Jimmy for another hole and see Mick hole a twenty-footer for par. 'I'm on fuckin' fire!' he declares.

I give Mick a thumbs up and agree he is indeed on fire, before I move on to join a single playing the next hole.

Michael cuts a dashing figure with a man-bun sticking out the top of his golf visor, a stand bag over his shoulder and a strong tattooed arm carrying the obligatory stubby holder and beer. He is superbly dressed, with a designer floral (non-golf) sports shirt untucked over comfortable trousers as he coolly assesses his next shot through dark Ray-Bans. It is a fashionable ensemble, clearly assembled with care and enjoyment. He wanted to look good and feel confident on the golf course. And he did. It is also evident he is a beginner struggling with his technique, but has enough pricey equipment to suggest the golf bug has bitten hard and he is determined to get good.

Michael is a fantastic addition to the game, the sort of individual who golf needs. But could he play at any of Sydney's private clubs in this attire? Unlikely. The untucked shirt would earn an instant scolding, and the visible tattoos and man-bun would be a magnet for reproachful side-eye.

It is no surprise then that Michael's favourite thing about Bondi is, 'You can get on here anytime.'

Next, I spot a couple of young guys hauling a bunch of elaborate fishing gear across the fairway. They make their way down a track that leads to the base of the cliffs and the crashing surf below. When they disappear down the path, I turn to some nearby golfers, who are also looking on, and ask what they're doing.

'Yeah, spearfishing! Beautiful spot down there,' one of the golfers replies. (I would later learn his name is Christian.) 'I do it myself sometimes.'

Christian and his mate Daniel are quintessential young eastern suburbs locals. They carry themselves with that easy-going surfer energy that is instantly friendly and completely without prejudice. And like many golfing surfers, they have an innate athleticism when it comes to hitting a golf ball. Strong grip, powerful shoulder turn and perfect balance – they've never joined a golf club or held a handicap, but they'd surely be low single figures with a bit of short-game practice. I watch them both rip driver off the 5th, Bondi's only par-4 and a hole that really should be famous (or infamous).

Bondi's entire nine holes occupy a tiny rectangle of grass along the clifftops at the northern end of the world-famous beach. Whoever designed it had a tough decision – zig-zag up and down the coast to get as many tees and greens along the cliff edge as possible, or splurge damn near all that beautiful coastline on one spectacular hole.

Bondi's unknown architect chose the latter and in so doing created the par-4 5th along possibly the most expensive 277-metres of golf real estate in the world.

A generous imagination might see the hole as a mirror of Cypress Point's 17th on the other side of the Pacific. Both holes ask the golfer to go left for safety or right along the cliff's edge. But unlike the beautiful stand of cypress at MacKenzie's seaside masterpiece, the obstacle dividing the 5th fairway at Bondi is a one hundred-foot tall sewer vent that can shroud the course with a stifling aroma in unfavourable winds.

After seeing Christian and Daniel smash a couple of power fades around the stink pipe, I wish them well and hang back on the tee to see who will come by next. Golf aside, it's an incredibly beautiful place to just sit and watch the ocean.

Soon enough, along comes a flinty old bloke named Brent. Brent had worked offshore but now lives nearby and gets out on the course whenever he can. He's right-handed but has always played golf left-handed for reasons he couldn't clearly explain. I tell him Phil Mickelson is also right-handed, which surprises and delights him.

'I'm a big Phil fan!' he exclaims. I suspect it also quietly justifies a choice he's been questioning his entire golfing life.

He carries his clubs in a fantastic old black-and-red Proline bag, the type with the rounded rectangle tube. He can't understand my enthusiasm for it. 'This old thing?' he says, holding up the bag incredulously, 'I've had it in the garage for years ... it's good is it?'

'Yes, it is,' I assure him, and speculate that certain golfing hipsters would pay good money for it. I can tell he is sceptical and maybe even starting to doubt my information on Mickelson's natural hand.

'So, what do you like about playing here?' I ask.

'Well, you can always get a game.' A recurring theme.

'I saw my wife off on a plane this morning, she's visiting our daughter. I came straight out here for a hit. And I tell you what, I won't be cooking tonight! Bloody good chef in the Diggers Club over there. Sri Lankan fella, that's where I'll be eating.'

I would later confirm for myself that the food is very good at the Diggers Club.

I watch Brent take on the tee shot at the 5th. As a leftie with a strong right side, it sets up easily for him. Aim straight at the stink pipe, fade it into the fairway and off he goes.

It's getting late and I start back to the clubhouse. There's a couple walking their dog, and a middle-aged man trying out his new drone. There's a couple of girls walking across several fairways to find a place to sit on the rocks and other non-golfers here and there, strolling, chatting or just looking out over the ocean.

I see a group of women in tracksuits and activewear finishing their round. Another woman is in full golf gear, introducing her non-golfer boyfriend to the game. They're sharing her set and enjoying the afternoon.

The conclusion of a tense four-ball match is unfolding at the 9th green, with the first round of drinks riding on a tricky five-footer. It misses, and two of the four start jumping and screaming in a way that is entirely familiar to anyone who has won a match where the stakes literally couldn't be lower, but also couldn't be higher.

I'm about to leave when I notice a young bloke walking off the course without finishing. 'Had enough?' I ask him.

'Nah, it was a bit busy out there, so I thought I'd just come back to the first,' he explains. 'Might have a beer on the balcony and jump back on the course when there's a gap.'

His name is James and he's been playing golf for a few years. His dad bought him a set of clubs that sat in the garage until it was a waste not to use them. Now he's hooked and plays all the public courses in the area: Bondi, Randwick, Moore Park, Woollahra. He's just back from a trip up the central coast playing Kooindah Waters and Magenta Shores, and he's convinced a group of mates to fly down to Barnbougle Dunes in a few weeks.

'What do you like about Bondi?' I ask.

He looks around and gives it some thought. 'Nobody here cares if you're shit.'

Diversity in golf is about letting new golfers know they're welcome in traditionally unwelcoming places. Bondi is anything but unwelcoming.

Words are powerful. Particularly simple ones.

'Wear what's comfortable.'

'You can get on anytime.'

'Nobody cares if you're shit.'

DON PLACEK

INTERVIEWED BY WILLIAM WATT
PHOTOGRAPHY BY NOAH JURIK
ORIGINAL ARTWORKS BY DON PLACEK

'There's been a core number of people who have always had an appetite for golf architecture, but I think it's doubled, or tripled, or quadrupled in a really short period of time, and that's exciting.'

DON PLACEK

Some artists work in oils, others in watercolour. Don Placek works in fairways and bunkers, bringing golf courses to life through his distinctive cyanotype maps. These striking blue-and-white prints are more than just course guides; they're love letters to the game's architectural heritage, each careful line revealing the soul of a golf course.

In an era where technology often threatens to overshadow tradition, Don Placek stands as a quiet guardian of golf's artistic roots. His journey began as a caddie, learning the game from the ground up, reading the subtleties of the land one loop at a time. This proved invaluable when he joined Renaissance Golf as a designer, where he continues to shape courses with the same attention to detail he brings to his maps.

But there's playfulness behind the precision. Take his Emoji Scoring System – a charming rebellion against the stern formality of traditional scorecards. For Placek, golf speaks its own visual language: the satisfied grin of a well-struck iron, the winking acknowledgment of a lucky bounce or the tearful joy of a career-best round.

It's an interesting dynamic, one person on coffee, the other on beer.

Don Placek: Yeah. They're both important, but the timing of the two is really critical.

So, prior to golf, what was your first introduction to visual arts?

It really started early on for me. I was really lucky. I grew up with my mum and dad constantly encouraging my two younger sisters and I to just try everything. You never know what'll be interesting and you really never know what you're good at, and that remains the case today. My mum was a schoolteacher and my dad was a golf professional. So the golf part came from my dad, and my mum always had access to a Big Chief tablet, a new box of crayons, and all those things that you need when you just want to learn.

Then Christmas would come, and maybe I'd get some pastels from Santa Claus, or I'd get a new box of pencils and charcoal, and I got to try it all. I was inspired by a blank page and thinking up something to draw – it didn't matter to me what it was. The golf part just became more and more prominent in my life as I began to play the game. Over time, the two things just kind of married themselves together. My parents encouraged all of us to try everything at least once. They didn't have much luck with me eating vegetables, but as far as drawing on paper and pad and canvas, that definitely resonated.

I've got an eighteen-month-old son who is just entering that phase where we're trying to figure out what he's interested in. Just this week, I discovered a band called Hermanos Gutiérrez, a guitar duo originally out of Ecuador. And to my surprise, he loves them and has become obsessed with guitar music. He only says a few dozen words, and 'guitar' is the most prominent of them. We've dug out my wife's guitar and he can strum away on that along with them – we want to encourage him to explore that as much as he wants.

Couldn't agree with you more, and what a lovely gift that music is. I mean, that's something I share with my colleagues and has been a big part of my life. Anytime I'm drawing, there's always some music on, and it goes back to my parents again. My dad listened to the Moody Blues and Johnny Cash, and threw in some Barry Manilow. Just being around it, you almost become part of what you're exposed to, and that's why it's so important to expose young people to as much as you can, because of that power. It almost happens by default in some ways, but good for you. Your young son is in good hands.

Funny you mention Johnny Cash. I've been listening to Rick Rubin's book The Creative Act *recently, I'm not sure if you've come across it?*

As it turns out, I have a copy right here on my desk! It's fantastic, isn't it?

Yes. There are so many nuggets in there that immediately resonate, as if I already knew that but had never heard it put so clearly before.

It's really, really well done. It's fascinating what the creative process is, and even those people who we acknowledge as being powerfully creative, particularly in his area of musicians and singer songwriters that just ... They get blocks too. Even the most creative people. Rick's just trying to help them get out of their own way in a lot of ways. It's an amazing book – it's one of those you can open up to any page and start reading and there's something for you.

For me it speaks to the relationship between being creative and the spirituality of golf. We are trying to design and realise golf holes that will inspire people to play and try shots they haven't before. We want them to have to overcome challenges, get themselves out of trouble, recover and sometimes even fail. And to do that, it is a creative and fluid process. The more comfortable you get with that, and not be too structured or rigid in your processes, the better job you're able to do.

Interesting. I hadn't really thought about how that book might apply in your field of golf course design and the visual work you do. One of the concepts of the book that I really like is it takes a bit of the pressure off as a creative person by talking about the fact that a lot of these ideas are just floating around in the ether or whatever you want to call it. They're quite mysterious in a way, but they come and they go, and you don't necessarily have to feel that everything you create has to be completely original, dug out from your soul. You can draw on those things that are around you and let it flow – you are almost just someone who is there to deliver that idea. Do you think that is what's happening with the resurgence in the interest and implementation of high-quality golf course architecture at the moment?

I think it's certainly a component of it. Also the iconic books by Alistair McKenzie, A W Tillinghast, George Thomas and others are more accessible. Today, you can get a dozen books that are really pertinent, and that anyone who's interested in golf course architecture not only should read, but would really enjoy. You can get them on Amazon for fifteen dollars in paperback now, whereas twenty-five years ago, there were maybe a hundred copies of the hardback version – they were almost antiques and you just couldn't get your mitts on them.

Couple that with what drone photography has done for golf architecture – just being able to convey what a golf course is really clearly and beautifully. When I grew up, it was only really the *World Atlas of Golf* that had an axonometric view. The idea was you could really get a feel for what was going on overall, especially with routings and seeing how a routing took advantage of a property. How could the routing tour you around the property to show you not just eighteen holes of golf, but hopefully what the land was like, what the vegetation was like, and what you could see looking offsite, which never shows up in a plan view drawing anywhere.

So it seems like all the planets have aligned themselves for people to not just discover this interest but really pursue it. There's been a core number of people who have always had an appetite for golf architecture, but I think it's doubled, or tripled, or quadrupled in a really short period of time, and that's exciting.

Can you talk us through the use of cyanotype in your plans?

I've always been interested in map making. There's something about following an eighteen-hole routing in a map that's almost like a treasure map. Where does it lead you? What's next? Do you go here next, or over there?

The cyanotype is an early photography technique developed in the late 1840s and 1850s by Sir John Herschel and was really one of the first ways to make prints.

It was a reverse reading. The natural background was this really deep denim, hued sky blue with a white contrast of line work. And for the work I do, it's all about the contrast – that's what really gets your attention and draws your eye. And it happens that cyanotype was state-of-the-art during the golden age of golf design, so it was used as part of the design process of many famous golf course designs.

Today, we use it more to convey a feeling of vintage – as with anything, what's old is new again. It doesn't matter if it's clothes or music or cars, whatever. Again, golf is no exception. It really speaks to me too because I think so much of the time I've been at Renaissance and all the fellas who I've had the great pleasure to work with, we're always trying to age stuff quickly, especially out in the field.

We want it to look like it's been there a really long time, and we want to cover our tracks. We don't want to leave any evidence that it was built – it was more found. This idea translates to the drawings too. We want to make them feel found.

So going backwards and studying how things were done is really why the cyanotype drawing I think resonates with me. I guess it's got a little of that treasure map feel to it as well.

It is also worth mentioning that a plan is a jumping off point. Sometimes they're really just a beginning. They're a stepping stone to what gets built. We feel strongly that the best stuff was done when people had to be creative and didn't have the physical resources or the money to make big changes to the property that was going to become golf. So they had to figure out ways to do it without the muscle of earthmoving equipment, and do it in a way that could be maintained at a number that made sense. So our plans are not prescriptive.

Could you take me through your creative process and some of the layering that goes into the final artwork?

Layering is the key word. It's a layered process because most of the work I do, I do in pencil first and conjure the ideas in quite a free way. I try to figure out the context, the style, the composition, and orient the plan in a way that's a little more interesting than just north always being up.

From there my favourite medium to use is ink on Mylar. It is really versatile and it allows you to take your back-of-the-napkin idea and put it into a more permanent form, going from pencil to ink. Because the Mylar is a transparent material, it drinks in the ink and really hangs onto it in a way that paper does not. I just love ink. I love the smell of it. I love how it adheres to the Mylar. I like the durability of it. It's as close to archival as you can get with something that you create with your hand.

Way back in the day, thirty years ago when I worked for the Dye family when I was still in college, we were doing all that work by hand using Mylar. And it's just always appealed to me ever since. I love working with it.

Once you've created those layers and built up your drawing, is it then a high-resolution scan that you go through, and is there any kind of post-production that then occurs?

Over the years I've learned that anytime you're going to reproduce something in any kind of quantity, is that if you start large and reduce it down, it gets tighter, cleaner and easier on the eyes. So I tend to draw well outside of whatever the intended proportions are going to be.

So if you're looking to create something at 8 x 10, I've probably started with it at more like 24 x 36. That way when it gets reproduced, it holds its detail and it doesn't get grainy or foggy or melt away. So that larger original work will go into a high-resolution digital scan that is then the main file we work off. That digital file can then be used in whatever form we would like to promote the project, or the golf course or the club. The great part is these days, once you have a quality image, it's limitless what you can do with it. You can put it on a towel, a golf bag, a piece of clothing. It can be a mural on a wall or a 5 x 7 postcard and everything in between. If you start with something that can be reinterpreted in many different ways, and it's a quality piece to begin with, you can go in many directions.

The client who commissioned the work usually gets the original, and we get that physically delivered to them. They often want to have the one thing that no one else has, or it's different in its own unique way, and it allows the client to do that.

You mentioned that the artwork is really a stepping off point for the way that Renaissance works. Does it ever get to a point where there are so many changes on the ground that you think – I might have to redraw this map?

In the early days and working for Tom [Doak], there was always this balance we were trying to strike between presenting something to a client at the beginning of a project. It couldn't be too detailed, because if it changes significantly during the process, people might think either we didn't do a good enough job planning, or that we didn't know what we were doing at the start. So yes, we had to be cognisant of the idea that you don't want to get too detailed too early.

Today, though, Renaissance has been doing it our way long enough now that the clients who we're lucky enough to have are more savvy. They understand how we work.

One of the most fascinating things that I'm involved in now is doing course guides for clubs after the course has been built. And you can see very clearly how different the hole ends up being realised in the field than it was conceptually at the beginning. Creating a golf hole is not unlike making a painting – you keep doing it until it's right. Sometimes it's a very quick process, and other times it takes an awful long time.

Some of the overhead views of the stuff we've done lately as it's realised and grassed, it's just wild to see the different forms that take shape. A lot of that is because, more so than ever, we are trying to hide the grassing lines – those transitions from fairway to rough or native areas – behind soft contours, so that your eye is not distracted. It allows the golfer to really pay attention to the way the ground moves, not where the grass starts and stops.

Can you tell me a little about your days as a caddie, and how that experience affected the way you see golf today?

Caddying was a huge part of my life. I was very fortunate to receive an Evans Scholarship to the University of Colorado Boulder, which paid my way for four years of school. I lived in a house with fifty-five other caddies who were in the same financial situation that I was. It was fantastic, and I'm really grateful for that experience to this day.

I learned a lot. If I have any people skills, well I learned a lot of my people skills from my parents and my family. But you also learn them when you get a loop and you're standing on the 1st tee about to work for somebody for four or five hours that you've never met before. You don't know how good they are at golf. You don't know how they play. You don't know what their expectations are.

It's wildly interesting. Every day is a job interview for a job where you don't even know what the requirements are. So you figure it out as you go, and you learn to take in quickly what your player is really after that day. Some people don't want you to say a word. Other people want oceans of information. It's engaging human interaction, and it is life-skill building.

Then figuring out how to get somebody around the golf course, hopefully playing maybe a little better than they would have otherwise, is the goal. You want to make the game fun, and playing well is a lot more fun than not. So anything you can do to help your player save a shot here and there, find a ball they didn't think they were going to. All those little things add up. It's a group of little gifts that you're giving to somebody.

It also helps you realise people hit the ball an infinite number of ways. They'll hit it sideways, and on the rare occasion, even backwards, somehow. And that's really important as an architect to bear in mind. You can get caught up on certain types of shots and things you want to offer up or challenge, but gosh, everybody hits it everywhere.

The more you can keep someone in the game, which is really what you're doing as a caddie too, that's when golf is really fun. There's nothing more demoralising than being out of play two seconds after you just started a brand-new hole. You just want to be in play off the tee.

If you can help your player as a caddie do that consistently, they're going to have way more fun. We try and design golf holes that challenge you certainly, but keeping as many people in the game for as long as you can, that's important too. It's probably one of the things I learned from caddying and then again working with Tom and the fellows, that's really important to us.

> 'We try and design golf holes that challenge you certainly, but keeping as many people in the game for as long as you can, that's important too.'

What is the Emoji Scoring System?

When I first met my lovely wife, Elizabeth, we talked about golf and that I was in the business of golf design and her face just sunk. I could see her thinking, *Oh no, I can't play golf very well, this might not go very well* kind of thing. She said, 'I have to be honest with you. Here's how I play golf. If I hit a good shot or have a good hole, I draw a happy face on the card. And if I don't, I draw a sad face. Sometimes I'll draw a confused face. And maybe the happy face isn't because I had a good score, but because I hit one really good shot on that hole.' From that point on, I knew this woman could be for me, because she's making golf fun.

Golf is hard. It's hard to play well for eighteen consecutive holes and string eighteen good holes together. The Emoji Scoring System immediately takes the seriousness out of it and settles you quickly. It's a great way to introduce people to the game – you want to make that really good first impression. It goes hand in hand with the real attention short courses are now getting – it's more manageable because it's more fun. And boy, is fun critical.

The Emoji Scoring System focuses on what's important – enjoyment, comradery and being outside and all the other great things about the game. At Old Barnwell, South Carolina, the idea of using the emoji scorecard for the kids' course has been kicked around. I love the idea because when you can introduce someone at an early age to the game, where they can grasp it and then travel with it the rest of their lives, you're really giving them a gift. Golf is one of the greatest gifts you can give to a young person. And if it's fun, you have a much better chance of them giving it a whirl.

I hope it takes off and we see the emoji scorecard become something that, as you say, junior golfers can use to introduce themselves to the game and take some of that pressure off that initial experience with the game. I remember playing when I was young and you'd get down on yourself and you'd get annoyed, and there's just no need for that really.

Right. It's human, but the quicker you can get out of your own way, the more fun you'll have. It's part of growing up, I think. We've got this special opportunity with such a global focus on golf at the moment, and if we can send out the right message to everybody, the game has got a great chance of being around for a lot longer. I'm working on a project for Chicago Golf Club for its course history, and we're trying to distil the essence of the template holes. What is the essence of the Redan, the Biarritz, the Short, the Eden, the Cape? What is the core idea of each one, in its most simplistic form? I've got a quote in here from the book that I'll leave you with: *'Making the simple, complicated is commonplace. But making the complicated simple, awesomely simple, that's creativity.'*
Charles Mingus

IONA — INHERENT ISOLATION

THE HEBRIDES, SCOTLAND

WORDS AND PHOTOGRAPHY
BY CLYDE JOHNSON

A diverse collection of islands to the west of mainland Scotland lie sparsely populated, if at all. At the mercy of Celtic, Norse and English occupation over a storied and long history, The Hebrides possess an almost mythical standing and still retain a character of their own. Overhearing the shipping forecast on a muffled radio in the background is perhaps the closest one would ever get to understanding life here, on the furthest edge of the earth.

For an Englishman based in St Andrews, the adventure would usually begin with a three-plus hour drive from coast-to-coast. On this trip, I took a diversion to pick up my fiancée from the Central Belt – a partner is always recommended for such an escapade. That, and the winding road north from Glasgow, which takes in a series of charming lochs. So too the Trossachs, a stunning area of wooded glens and braes.

Not far south of Oban hides the least detached of the Slate Islands in The Inner Hebrides, the isle of Seil. Down a backroad and over a seemingly innocuous humpbacked span takes you to 'The Bridge over the Atlantic'. Seil, if anything, is best known for its slate – certainly not for its cosy nine-holer, which doesn't appear on any map I have ever seen. Unexpected discoveries like these can be the best, even if an unscheduled round is a no-go. A quick hop over a fence reveals that two-thirds of the course sits along a boat-filled bay. With one bridge between them, three parched greens are dotted either side of a tidal inlet.

At this point, the first ferry ride will have to wait until the morning. Luckily, the island gateway of Oban is filled with bed and breakfasts, as well as the funky-looking 4452-yard Glencruitten. I'll be back with clubs for that one too.

The next morning, fifty minutes along the sea, over to the Isle of Mull, brings a change in pace. A right turn and short drive take us to the next nine at Craignure, which tracks over a paddock that

protrudes into sheltered waters, though the compact course offers the odd hint of typically Scottish ingenuity. Tucked attractively between a rocky shoulder and the Sound of Mull, Ben Nevis – Scotland's highest Monro – wouldn't be the worst line when pitching to the squared second green.

Most island-hoppers head straight for the colourful fishing port of Tobermory, but a loop around the Mull's northerly half is rewarded by a paddle at Calgary Bay (on a sunny summer's day, at least). Clambering without regard to visibility, the island's main nine tackles heathery, deep rolls, arduous inclines and even sharper descents. High above Tobermory's steeply banked houses, and with cross-Sound views to the most desolate of mainland coastlines, the exertion is appropriately compensated.

With each of the nines completed, there is more undiscovered perimeter to experience: a single track, with sparsely distributed passing points. Fionnphort is our end goal, and a generously proportioned car park lets us know we've reached the south-west tip of Mull.

With only the resident population of 125 or so allowed to drive on Iona, the remaining crossing is made mostly by a hoard of pedestrians. This brings an inevitable interaction, as one set of tourists exchanges their place with another. On this occasion, it's a local who catches our attention, or rather, that I catch the local's attention. 'Off for a round today, pal?' (I suspect not many make the crossing with a golf bag on their shoulder, let alone know that a course even exists on the tiny island.)

It could have been a different story.

A couple of months earlier, after a day exploring Tom Doak's routing for his new St Patrick's Links at Rosapenna in Ireland, Doak and I were sharing an evening jaunt around the Atlantic Drive. Its stark, rugged beauty must have jogged his mind to the two courses he'd still like to see on the British Isles: 'Whalsay (on the Shetland Isles) ... and Iona'.

'There's a golf course on Iona?' My excited response. Lucky this trip had already been planned, and Iona was the one island my non-golfing partner wanted to visit.

First, we make our way to the tiny Post Office building, just off the slipway on the right. Squeezed between its corrugated metal walls, we purchase our scorecard, with a sterling pound covering the green fee too. With the day turning danker and a sea mist drawing in, the golf would need to wait. One mile wide and four miles deep, rental pushbikes turned out to be the ideal way to make a first pass of the island. From the village of Baile Mòr, there are, to our surprise, two slightly different routes, for at least part of the journey west. A gate signals that it is time to hop-off and push. This looks like it should be the course, though a thickening haar tries to convince otherwise. The sound of gently lapping waves as our feet rolled over a pebbly beach couldn't deceive that we'd reached the 'Bay at the Back of the Ocean'. Tracking along the high point of brightly toned, built-up deposits reveals an eroded threshold of sandy soils, partially stabilised by a smattering of thistles. Inland and just discernible, the wind-tattered remains of a flag.

But we are, of course, there to see the abbey. A worthy structure, it's perhaps most impressive that the site has survived as the centre of Christianity since St Columba's arrival in 563 AD, despite attempted Viking raids, not to mention the Protestant Reformation of the 1500s.

Further exploration of the smidgey, sandy beaches of Iona's relatively sheltered east flank allows time for the cloud to break, and the clock to wind down. From the north of the village's smattering of settlements, a gravelly path through farm and fields shortens the return trip on foot. Thankfully, for me at least, the long, drawn-out daylight hours of Scotland comfortably cater to a 7:30 pm tee-off. Through the gate again, with visibility this time unobscured, even the experienced eye questions if this is really golf.

An expanse of sheep-mown fescue, nourished at almost uniform height, provides a fine playing surface, though there is little clue as to where play should begin, or follow. It could be anywhere, and the landscape is perfectly suited to those with a spirit of adventure. But it might be my only time here, so I must lean on the local wisdom. The scorecard, suddenly worth way more than that spare change in my pocket, directs to a small concrete block on the rise to the right, faded white, with a red '1' – this must be it, though I still have little clue, with 180-degrees worth of

undefined ground. Trusting the card, and with a little of my own instinct, I drive over the trackway and burn, before approaching blindly over a furrowed rise. Finally, the flag in view.

Two more flags, barely perceptible in their weather-ravaged state, flutter in the distance. I'm away, the golf-navigable land hemmed by rises of granite. Part-way up the southerly bookend, the par-3 3rd green is perched beyond a diagonal sand scrape. With nature its shaper, this blowout sprawls at the mercy of the wind. Play too strong, and your ball is in the power of a rocky ricochet.

Turning back, and aided by the elevation, the full beauty of this rarefied golfing tract is revealed. It's not just sheep-rutted trails and thistle that break up the links land – a small rocky knoll must be carried over or tracked around on route to the 4th green. Mowed out on a three-metre radius – perhaps once a summer month at most – it's not just printing costs that your green fee goes towards.

The beach is in play for the next two holes, until a wire fence signifies an inland incursion. A longish-three up-and-over into a saucer follows, though the boundary is neither out-of-bounds nor historically territorial – the Machar has long been shared by crofters. North of the sheep-managing barbs brings contour more commonly associated with seaside golf, with the 9th green slanting-off a dune-like ridge.

It's a brief, rumply encounter, with a rocky plinth hosting the starting point of the back nine. Having eaten up a stretch of pastoral ground into the prevailing wind, the 10th green angles behind and between opposing fescue-sprinkled upstands of rock. As my accomplice disappears over the sharper inclines to the right, the next scene is otherworldly: protrusions of Lewisian Gneiss on land and into sea. Again, the 11th green is sheltered between the hard stuff, only this time, at the end of a long three playing blind over a crest. One for the locals (and I don't mean the grazing sheep), there would be a chance to safely steer one in behind with the slope from right to left. But not too far right, for a quaint, white-sanded beach hides beyond it.

It would be easy to get lost as a long par-4 bends around a crater and shoulder combination on its transition back into the dunescape. Heading towards what I suspect to be atypically quiet waters, the ridge-to-ridge 14th appears less frightful as the evening light softens. From there, I negotiate a hollow of gnarly marram on the way to a saddled green.

The descent from that slight highpoint initially crosses back over the 15th approach and two fence lines. Nestled behind a dune, the 16th green blindly tumbles away towards a further fence corner. Such quirks give Iona's course a sense of scale among the expanse of low-fertile ground.

Back to the water, it is a distinctly undefined jaunt over the final two, but one that has to be made quickly with seductively fading light and another couple of miles back to our austere accommodation.

This most definitely is golf, in its purest imaginable form.

Acknowledgements

This book is dedicated to the real custodians of the game: the golden age golf course architects, both old and new. The deeper I dig into golf, the more layers of wisdom I seem to uncover. Much of it has been lying in the earth for centuries, waiting to be dug up, and I'm grateful to the architects who embedded it so deeply, as well as those who continue to champion the essence of the game today and make their own mark.

To all our contributors – thank you for answering the call (or many emails) and for lending your creativity, insights and wisdom to this book. Your passion for the game helps fuel my fire and I love learning from you all.

To Jack O'Sullivan for your considered work with the Contours brand, Ben Jarvis for your advice and guidance for the London Heathlands piece, and to the Melbourne golf community at large who continue to support my work with such generosity.

To Pam Brewster for your guidance and support for this latest project, Murray Batten for bringing Contours to life in print, and the rest of the brilliant team at Hardie Grant who understood the vision from day one.

To my friends and family, and especially Rosie and Winston, thank you for the words of encouragement and the endless support. Your patience during the long editing sessions and understanding when 'just one more research trip' was required.

Finally, to the golfers who appreciate that the ground beneath our feet tells the greatest stories of all. I'll see you out on the links.

About the author

William Watt is a Melbourne-based photographer, writer and the founder of *Caddie Magazine*. Since launching the publication in 2016, he has established himself as one of golf's most distinctive voices, combining stunning visual storytelling with deep architectural knowledge to document the world's most remarkable golf destinations. His work has taken him across six continents, from Scotland's remote links to the Himalayan foothills, capturing both the strategic brilliance and natural beauty of golf course design.

Watt's first book, *Lofted: Remarkable & Far-flung Adventures for the Modern Golfer* (Hardie Grant Books, 2020), compiled the best stories from *Caddie's* early editions into a celebrated 264-page journey through golf's most extraordinary landscapes. Through Contours Agency, Watt provides photography, branding and content services to the world's finest golf courses, working closely with renowned architects, clubs and destinations to uncover golf's deeper stories.

Published in 2025 by Hardie Grant Books, an imprint of Hardie Grant Publishing

Hardie Grant Books (Melbourne)
Wurundjeri Country
Level 11, 36 Wellington Street
Collingwood, Victoria 3066

Hardie Grant North America
2912 Telegraph Ave
Berkeley, California 94705

hardiegrant.com/books

Hardie Grant acknowledges the Traditional Owners of the Country on which we work, the Wurundjeri People of the Kulin Nation and the Gadigal People of the Eora Nation, and recognises their continuing connection to the land, waters and culture. We pay our respects to their Elders past and present.

A catalogue record for this book is available from the National Library of Australia

Contours
ISBN 978 1 76145 166 9

10 9 8 7 6 5 4 3 2 1

Publishing Director: Pam Brewster
Head of Editorial: Jasmin Chua
Editor: Elizabeth Turner
Creative Director: Kristin Thomas
Designer: Murray Batten
Head of Production: Todd Rechner
Production Controller: Elly Cridland

Colour reproduction by Splitting Image Colour Studio
Printed in China by Leo Paper Products LTD.

MIX
Paper | Supporting responsible forestry
FSC® C020056

The paper this book is printed on is from FSC®-certified forests and other sources. FSC® promotes environmentally responsible, socially beneficial and economically viable management of the world's forests.

Front cover: Sunrise on the 6th green at Te Arai Links, South Course
Back cover: Sunset on the 7th and 4th greens at Te Arai Links, North Course

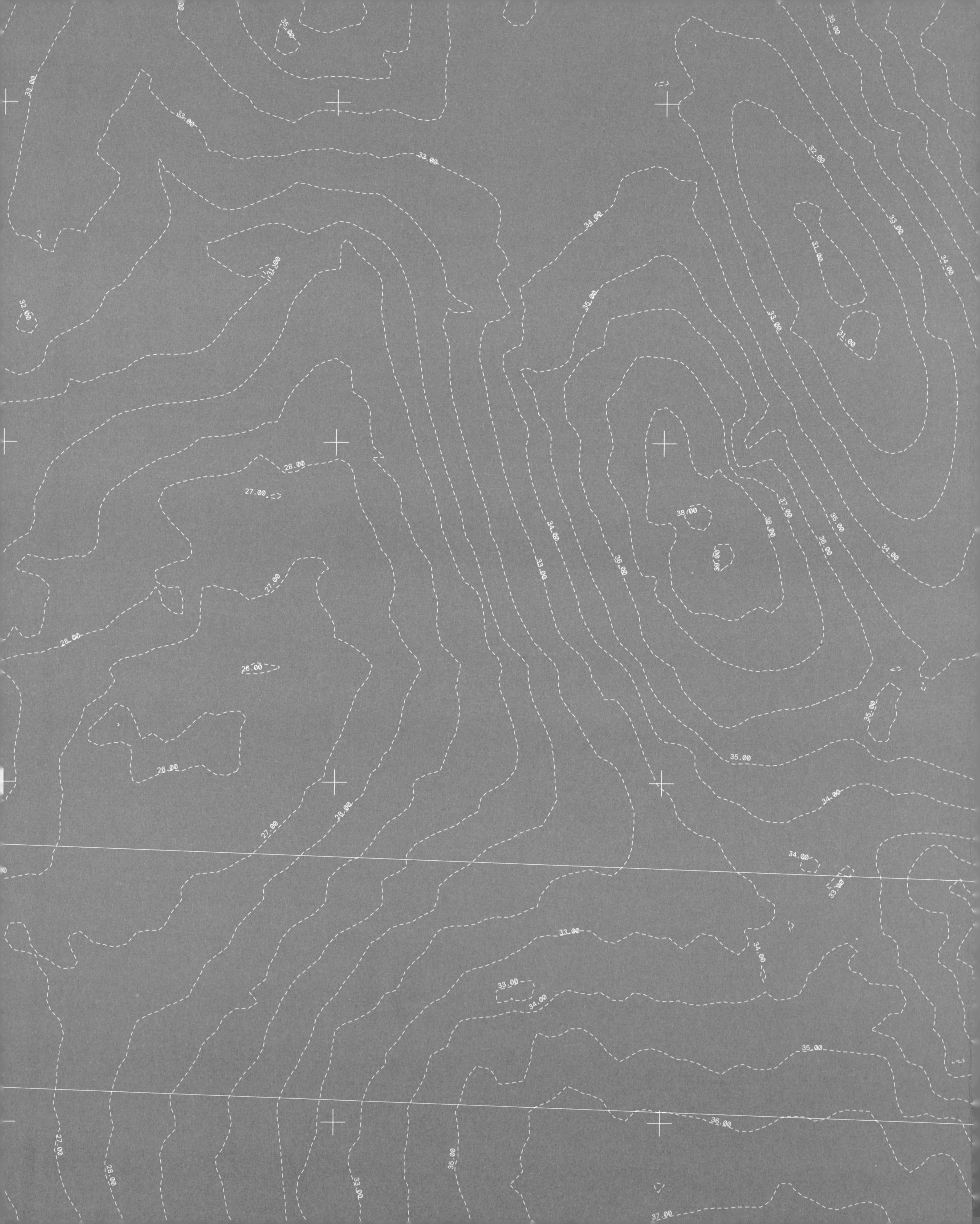
35.00
33.00
33.00
33.00
35.00
32.00
34.00
33.00
31.00
34.00
35.00
33.00
31.00
28.00
27.00
38.00
37.00
38.00
35.00
36.00
34.00
33.00
39.00
27.00
28.00
26.00
35.00
26.00
35.00
34.00
28.00
27.00
34.00
33.00
33.00
34.00
33.00
34.00
35.00
36.00
27.00
36.00
28.00
33.00
37.00